AN UNOFFICIAL GUIDE TO *BATTLE ROYALE*

101 EXTREME SURVIVAL TECHNIQUES FOR FORTNITERS

MASTER COMBAT SERIES #4

JASON R. RICH

Sky Pony Press
New York

Copyright © 2019 by Hollan Publishing, Inc.

Fortnite® is a registered trademark of Epic Games, Inc.

The Fortnite game is copyright © Epic Games, Inc.

Sky Pony Press books may be purchased in bulk at special discounts for sales promotion, corporate gifts, fund-raising, or educational purposes. Special editions can also be created to specifications. For details, contact the Special Sales Department, Sky Pony Press, 307 West 36th Street, 11th Floor, New York, NY 10018 or info@skyhorsepublishing.com.

Sky Pony® is a registered trademark of Skyhorse Publishing, Inc.®, a Delaware corporation.

Visit our website at www.skyponypress.com.

10 9 8 7 6 5 4 3 2 1

Library of Congress Cataloging-in-Publication Data is available on file.

Cover design by Brian Peterson
Cover artwork by Getty Images
Interior photography by Jason R. Rich

Print ISBN: 978-1-5107-4974-0
E-Book ISBN: 978-1-5107-4979-5

Printed in China

TABLE OF CONTENTS

SECTION 1

ARE YOU READY TO EXPERIENCE
FORTNITE: BATTLE ROYALE?

SAVE THE WORLD

BATTLE ROYALE

100 PLAYER PVP

PLAY

CREATIVE

Without a doubt, *Fortnite: Battle Royale* is the world's most popular "battle royale" game on the PC, Mac, PlayStation 4, Xbox One, Nintendo Switch, iPhone, iPad, and Android-based mobile devices. The game has more than 250 million registered players (as of late-March 2019) and offers many unique ways to experience the combat-oriented action.

It's important to understand that when playing *Fortnite: Battle Royale*, there are no proven steps to follow that will allow you to achieve success during every match. There are always multiple ways to face the challenges encountered while on the island, but some will definitely work better than others. In general, fast reaction time, aiming accuracy, and having the most powerful selection of weapons and tools on hand will help lead you to victory!

*Like all battle royale games, during every match you participate in, your main focus should on two things—**combat** and **survival**. Simply select the **Press to Start** option to kick off your adventure!*

Each time you visit the mysterious island where matches take place, you'll need to successfully juggle a wide range of important responsibilities if you want to stay alive long enough to achieve #1 Victory Royale. To do this when playing the Solo game play mode, for example, up to 99 of your enemies must perish during the match and the soldier you're controlling must become the last person alive on the island.

To play Fortnite: Battle Royale (as opposed to Fortnite: Save the World) Select the **Battle Royale** option. Then, to remain alive during each match, there are many strategies you can and should adopt.

If you consider yourself to be a highly skilled gamer, it's possible to land on the island in the heart of a popular point of interest (location), grab a weapon, and immediately confront enemies in firefights. During the match, defeat as many enemy soldiers as possible while simultaneously exploring the island, avoiding the deadly storm, building and managing your arsenal, surviving enemy attacks, and skillfully executing your own attacks on enemies. Shown here, the soldier is about to embark on a dangerous quest into Neo Tilted (formally known as Tilted Towers).

Another approach you can adopt is to land in a remote and less-popular location on the island. Avoid enemy contact during the early stages of a match, and spend time building up your arsenal, as you begin preparing for the End Game (the final minutes of a match when only a few soldiers remain alive).

Fortnite: Battle Royale Offers Multiple Game Play Modes

Whatever your gaming style, *Fortnite: Battle Royale* offers a handful of different game play modes that allow you to experience the high-intensity combat action on your own, with a partner, as part of a four-soldier squad, or as a member of 50-soldier team, for example.

*In addition to the **Solo**, **Duos**, **Squads**, **Playground**, and **Creative** game play modes that are always available, Epic Games often introduces limited-time game play modes that offer a wide range of unique challenges.*

The **Solo** game play mode pits your soldier against 99 others, each being controlled in real time by a different gamer. Your objective is to be the last soldier alive at the end of a match.

The **Duos** game play mode allows you to team up with one gamer to take on up to 98 other enemies on the island. You and your partner must work together, share weapons and resources, and launch well-coordinated attacks to achieve #1 Victory Royale.

*The **Squads** game play mode provides the opportunity to team up with three other gamers to create a four-soldier squad that must defeat 24 other squads during a match to achieve #1 Victory Royale. As always, there's no second or third place. You either win the match or perish trying.*

*Check out the **Creative** game play mode if you want to custom design the island from scratch, and then set your own rules of engagement for when you and your fellow gamers participate in matches. You can also experience islands and challenges that other gamers have designed from scratch.*

Select **Creative** and then choose a specific scenario that someone else has created or choose the Start A Server option to design the island from the ground up and determine exactly what happens on it during each match.

Playground allows you to visit the mysterious island alone or with a few other gamers, but not participate in traditional matches. If you lose a firefight or get defeated, your soldier can respawn almost instantly. Use Playground mode to practice working with different types of weapons and tools, and safely explore the island at your own pace, without the fear of getting attacked, being forced into a combat situation, or having to outrun the storm.

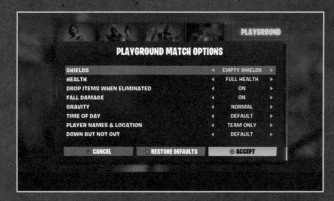

In **Playground** mode, you determine the rules of engagement and can customize the experience for each match.

When selecting either a **Duos** or **Squads** match, choose the **Fill** option to have the game choose your partner or squad mates. With this option selected, you'll be teamed up with random strangers. By selecting the **Don't Fill** option (shown here above the Accept button), you're able to choose online friends to be your partner or squad mates.

To invite one or more online friends to join you for a match, from the Lobby screen, one at a time, select a "+" icon that's displayed near the center of the screen, to the right or left of your soldier. Pick which friend(s) you want to invite from the menu displayed on the left side of the screen.

Select an online friend and choose the Join Party option to invite that person to be your partner (in a Duos match) or squad mate (in a Squads match).

While in the Lobby, if you see a yellow banner above one or more of the "+" icons that says, "[Player Name] Invited You!," these are invitations from your online friends. You're able to accept or deny an invitation to participate in a match. Accept one invitation at a time to join that gamer for a Duos or Squads match.

Customize Your Soldier's Appearance Before a Match

Prior to each match, you're able to customize your soldier's appearance and choose which six emotes you'll have access to during that match.

The outfit you choose for your soldier prior to a match helps to determine their appearance. By mixing and matching outfits, Outfit Styles, as well as a Back Bling and Harvesting Tool design, for example, you're able to give your soldier a unique appearance.

Solider customizations are done from the Locker. Select the Locker tab from the top of the Lobby screen, and then choose your soldier's outfit, Back Bling design, Harvesting Tool design, Glider design, Contrail design, emotes, and adjust the other customizable options.

Some Outfits Are Very Rare, While Others Are Extremely Common

Some outfits are classified as Legendary. These tend to cost the most, at around $20.00 (US) each, and are typically offered for a very limited time. Most (but not all) Legendary outfits come with a matching Back Bling design.

Other outfits are classified as Common, Uncommon, Rare, or Epic. Priced around 800 V-Bucks ($8.00 US), Common outfits are the least expensive and tend to get re-released within the Item Shop rather often. Outfits classified as Uncommon, Rare (shown above), and Epic are more expensive than Common outfits, but less expensive than Legendary outfits. Shown above is the Bandolette outfit. It's a Rare outfit that's part of the Tropic Troopers set. The price of this outfit is 1,200 V-Bucks (about $12.00 US).

Most newly released outfits are part of a set. The items in a set often include a matching Back Bling design, Harvesting Tool design, and/or a Glider design, although most items in a set are typically sold separately. Shown above is the Uncommon Whiplash outfit, priced at 800 V-Bucks (approximately $8.00 US).

Shown here is one of the many outfits that fall into the Rare category. It's called Marino and it's part of the Beach Battalion set. As you can see, this outfit comes bundled with matching Back Bling.

Depending on which gaming system you're using to play Fortnite: Battle Royale, in-game purchases of V-Buck bundles are done through that gaming system's online store. Shown here using a PS4, a bundle of 2,500 V-Bucks (plus 300 bonus V-Bucks) is being purchased from the PlayStation Store using the credit card linked to the account.

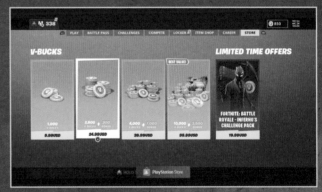

This Shadow Ops outfit is an example of an Epic outfit. It's part of the Stealth Syndicate set. Epic outfits typically cost 1,500 V-Bucks, or about $15.00 (US). It's important to understand that while outfits and related items can dramatically alter the appearance of your soldier, none offer any tactical advantage whatsoever during a match. These items are for cosmetic purposes only.

At least once or twice per gaming season, special bundle packs are offered from the Shop. These typically includes one limited edition and exclusive outfit, along with a small bundle of V-Bucks, and sometimes other goodies, all offered at a discounted price. The outfits offered through bundles are not sold in the Item Shop, and once the current gaming season ends, typically won't be offered ever again.

The items available to you from the Locker must either be purchased (using V-Bucks, which cost real money) or unlocked by completing challenges while playing Fortnite: Battle Royale. To make purchases, first visit the Shop and buy a bundle of V-Bucks (in-game currency). The more V-Bucks you purchase at once, the bigger the discount you receive.

In addition to purchasing items that allow you to customize your soldier, every gaming season, an optional **Battle Pass** can be purchased. A Battle Pass allows you to participate in 100 Tier-based challenges throughout the gaming season (which lasts approximately two to three months).

To purchase a Battle Pass or view the Tier-based challenges a Battle Pass includes, select the Battle Pass tab that's displayed along the top of the Lobby screen. Select the yellow Purchase button located near the bottom-left corner of the screen to acquire a new Battle Pass.

A basic Battle Pass is priced at 950 V-Bucks (about $9.50 US).

By completing Battle Pass challenges, you're able to unlock prizes, including items that allow you to customize your soldier's appearance. Once a new gaming season begins, old Battle Passes expire and a new one must be purchased. However, like items from the Item Shop, purchasing a Battle Pass is optional. Shown here, a bundle of 100 V-Bucks was unlocked as a prize for completing Tier 26 during Season 9's Battle Pass.

Upon completing Tier 27 during Season 9, the unlocked prize was a special Back Bling design that featured a robotic dog virtual pet that a soldier can carry around with them in their backpack during a match.

If you can't or don't want to complete specific Tier-based challenges after acquiring a Battle Pass, from the Battle Pass screen you can use V-Bucks to unlock one Tier at a time and instantly receive the prize associated with that challenge. The price to unlock each Tier is 150 V-Bucks, which is equivalent to about $1.50 (US).

Another thing you'll want to do before a match is tweak the game's settings, based on your experience as a gamer and your primary gaming style. To access the Settings menus, from the Lobby, select the Menu icon that's displayed in the top-right corner of the screen.

By selecting the Challenges tab, also displayed near the top-center of the Lobby screen, you can choose to participate in other types of Event, Daily, Weekly (shown here), or Style-based challenges that often do not require purchasing a Battle Pass, but that allow you to win prizes for completing each challenge.

When the Menu appears, select the gear-shaped Settings icon to access the Settings menus.

Select the Style tab from the Challenges screen to see specific outfits that have multiple Styles that can be unlocked by completing specific challenges. Once an outfit's Style is unlocked, select it from the Locker to alter the appearance of that outfit.

Along the top of the Settings screen are a selection of tabs. Click on the tabs, one at a time, to reveal a Settings-related submenu. When playing the PS4 version of Fortnite: Battle Royale, for example, these include: Game, Brightness, Audio, Accessibility, Input, Controller, and Account. How to adjust some of these settings and why doing this is useful for improving your speed and aim, for example, is covered within Section 2–Fortnite: Battle Royale Basics.

Consider Upgrading Your Gaming Gear

Once you start getting good at playing *Fortnite: Battle Royale*, if you want to give yourself an additional edge, especially in combat or when building (when speed and fast reflexes are essential), consider upgrading your gaming gear.

One equipment upgrade that'll prove very useful when playing a Duos or Squads match, for example, is a gaming headset. Sound effects play a major role in *Fortnite: Battle Royale*, and it's essential that you hear these sound effects as clearly as possible during matches.

If your soldier gets eliminated from a Duos or Squads match, or a temporary game play mode offered by Epic Games, your partner or a squad mate has the ability to revive your soldier during a match. This has to be done within about 90 seconds. Once a soldier is eliminated, one of their allies needs to grab that defeated soldier's Reboot Card. Being able to call for help and easily exchange information between squad members using a headset while a rescue is in progress is definitely beneficial.

Quickly bring the Reboot Card to a Respawn Van. These blue vans can be found throughout the mysterious island. Taking advantage of these vans allows you and your partner to potentially stay in matches longer and be able to work together to achieve #1 Victory Royale.

When playing a Solo match, consider connecting high-quality headphones to your gaming system. However, when playing a Duos or Squads match, you'll need to speak in real time with your partner or squad mates to plan perfectly timed attacks, for example. This can be done using an optional gaming headset, which has a built-in microphone. Shown here is the Cloud Alpha gaming headset ($99.99) from HyperX Gaming (www.hyperxgaming.com).

In addition to a gaming headset, if you're playing Fortnite: Battle Royale on a PC or Mac, you may be able to improve your reaction time and aiming precision by upgrading your computer keyboard and mouse with a gaming keyboard and mouse. Many companies, like HyperX Gaming (www.hyperxgaming.com), offer this type of optional gaming equipment. The HyperX Alloy Elite RGB keyboard ($139.99) is shown here.

PS4 and Xbox One gamers can connect a gaming keyboard and mouse to their console to control their soldier (as opposed to using a gaming controller). Another option is to upgrade your gaming controller to one designed specifically for pro gamers. For example, SCUF Gaming offers the SCUF Impact, which is an optional PS4 controller (priced around $165.00 US). To learn about other companies offering optional gaming equipment that can be used when playing Fortnite: Battle Royale, be sure to check out Section 4–Fortnite: Battle Royale Resources.

If you're a Nintendo Switch gamer, seriously consider upgrading to Nintendo's optional Pro Controller ($69.99) when playing Fortnite: Battle Royale, as opposed to using the Joy-Con controller that comes bundled with the gaming console.

Once you've selected your gaming equipment and have customized some of the options offered by the Settings menu, be sure to memorize the controls you'll need when playing. With plenty of practice, you'll develop your muscle memory for *Fortnite: Battle Royale*, so eventually, you won't have to waste valuable seconds thinking about what control, keyboard, or mouse button to press in order to control your soldier, select and fire a weapon, build, or use a Health or Shield replenishment item, for example.

As soon as you develop your muscle memory and can easily and quickly control the gaming action without thinking about it, your response time will improve, and you'll have a much easier time surviving longer and defeating more enemies with greater precision.

Mastering *Fortnite: Battle Royale* Takes Practice!

Regardless of the gaming equipment you're using, if you want to become a highly skilled *Fortnite: Battle Royale* gamer, it's going to take a lot of practice! However, you can save a lot of time discovering tips and strategies for winning firefights, using weapons, exploring, and building by reading this unofficial strategy guide.

Section 3—*101 Extreme Survival Techniques* is divided up into twelve sections to help you quickly discover strategies that'll help you master various aspects of this game. Even if you think you're a pro when playing other battle royale games, you'll quickly discover that *Fortnite: Battle Royale* offers a whole new and exciting set of gaming experiences, and each game play mode includes a vastly different set of challenges.

Just about every week, Epic Games releases a game update (patch) that adds new elements to the game, such as new points of interest, new weapons, new vehicles, and/or new Health and Shield replenishment items. Meanwhile, in conjunction with each new gaming season, you can expect some major changes to be made to the geography of the mysterious island, so there will be new points of interest to explore, as well as new challenges to overcome.

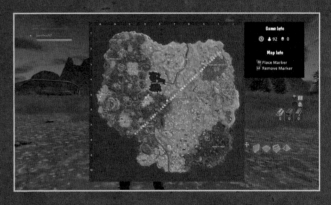

Shown here is what the Island Map looked like during Season 3.

Check out what the Island Map looked like a few months later, during Season 5.

This is what the Island Map looked like near the start of Season 9. As you can see, many points of interest have changed, and the climates found in different areas of the island have evolved as well. To become a highly skilled Fortnite: Battle Royale *gamer, it's essential to become well acquainted with the island's new terrain at the start of each gaming season, so you can use the terrain you're in at any given moment to your utmost advantage.*

Be Unpredictable and Expect the Unexpected

Of course, when experiencing a *Fortnite: Battle Royale* match, you also need to contend with the often-unpredictable actions of your enemies, each of whom is being controlled by another gamer in real time. Since you never know how your adversaries will react in specific situations, you need to always be ready for anything, and at the same time, as you're controlling your own soldier, move and act in unpredictable ways.

When your adversaries can anticipate what you're going to do next in a firefight, for example, this puts you at a huge disadvantage and often makes your soldier an easy target. Thus, it's important to keep moving in an unpredictable pattern, and figure out creative ways you can surprise your enemies with sneak attacks, ambushes, and clever ways to defend your soldier. Tips for how to do all of this are covered within *Section 3—101 Extreme Survival Techniques.*

Beyond the 101 fighting and survival techniques covered within this strategy guide, if you want to master various aspects of Fortnite: Battle Royale, be sure to check out the other full-color, unofficial guides in this Fortnite: Battle Royale **Master Combat** series written by Jason R. Rich and published by Sky Pony Press. To learn more about these books, which are sold separately, visit **www.FortniteGameBooks.com**.

SECTION 2

FORTNITE: BATTLE ROYALE BASICS

When playing *Fortnite: Battle Royale*, every match starts off in the Lobby. It's from here that you choose a game play mode.

If you'll be playing a Duos or Squads match, and you've chosen the **Don't Fill** option, from the Lobby you're able to accept invites to participate in matches with your online friends or extend your own invitations to others. As soon as you're ready to join a match, select the **Play** option from the Lobby. To play with strangers as your allies during a match, first choose the **Fill** option.

Get Ready to Ride the Battle Bus

After selecting the **Play** option, your solider gets transported automatically to the pre-deployment area. You'll hang out here for a few minutes while waiting for up to 99 other gamers to join the match.

While in the pre-deployment area you can explore, interact with other soldiers (using emotes), or collect weapons and practice shooting, for example. Anything you collect while in the pre-deployment area gets left behind once your soldier boards the Battle Bus.

The Battle Bus is a blue-colored flying bus that transports all 100 soldiers from the pre-deployment area to the mysterious island. There's just one catch . . . the Battle Bus does not land. Instead, as the bus is flying over the island, you must choose when your soldier should leap from the bus and freefall to the island.

As the Battle Bus is flying over the island, use the directional controls to look backward, behind the bus. You'll be able to see rival soldiers leap from the bus. Doing this can help you determine where the majority of the enemy soldiers will be landing.

Either while waiting in the pre-deployment area, or during your flight on the Battle Bus, consider checking the Island Map. You'll notice that a line, comprised of arrow icons, displays the random route the Battle Bus will be taking over the island, as well as the direction the bus will travel. Use this information to help you choose the perfect time to leap from the bus so you can reach your desired landing location.

Points of interest located near the very start of the route that the Battle Bus will take tend to be very popular, so when you land on the island, you're almost guaranteed to encounter enemy soldiers right away.

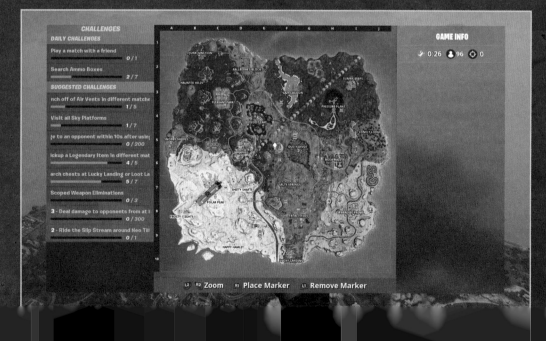

Destinations located at the very end of the Battle Bus's route also tend to be popular landing destinations. In this case, Frosty Flights (located between map coordinates A8 and B8) is a point of interest near the start of the route, and Sunny Steps (located near map coordinates I2.5) is the point of interest near the end of the route.

After leaping from the Battle Bus as it passed over Sunny Steps near the end of its route, this soldier activated his Glider as he approached land to ensure a safe landing. At this point during your soldier's descent, look for weapons lying on the ground, out in the open, so your soldier can land near those weapons and grab them quickly.

Remember, any time you land at a popular point of interest, you'll very likely encounter enemy soldiers right away. For this reason, it's essential that during your soldier's freefall, you guide them as quickly as possible to your desired landing spot. Do this by pointing your soldier straight downward, using the navigational controls.

You can also count on points of interest located near the center of the map always being popular landing spots. Other popular landing spots tend to be the newest points of interest that were most recently added to the map. At the start of Season 9, for example, Neo Tilted, Loot Lake, and Dusty Divot were among the popular locations found near the center of the Island Map.

If you're the first soldier to land at a specific location, you'll likely have a few seconds to quickly find and grab a weapon and ammo, so you can help your soldier protect themselves as rival soldiers land shortly after. However, when your soldier is not the first one to land at a particular spot (shown here), the risk of getting shot and eliminated from the match within seconds after landing increases dramatically. As you can see, the soldier who just landed remains unarmed, yet she's being shot at. Her elimination is just a second or two away.

To avoid encountering enemies as soon as you land, so you'll have time to find and gather weapons, ammo, and useful loot items, consider landing just outside of a popular point of interest. Shown here, the soldier landed on a hill located just outside of Neo Tilted. On this hill, weapons and loot items can often be found immediately upon landing. Once armed, the soldier can then descend into the popular Neo Tilted city.

During freefall, moments before your soldier is about to land on the island, their Glider will automatically deploy. This slows down their rate of descent and ensures a safe landing. When the Glider is activated, you'll have better navigational control, allowing you to choose a very precise landing spot.

Yet another option is to land in a remote area of the island, where you're not very likely to encounter enemy soldiers. You'll see come across plenty of structures and buildings that you can search and loot. This gives you even more time to explore and build up your soldier's arsenal. Especially on the outskirts of the island, as well as in between labeled points of interest on the map, there are many remote landing location options.

While you're still in the air, be on the lookout for weapons lying out in the open that your soldier can land near and quickly grab. If you spot the glow of a chest, that's even better. Chests contain multiple items that can include weapons, ammo, and other loot items, including items used to replenish your soldier's Health and Shield meters.

In addition to looking for weapons just prior to landing on the island, keep your eyes peeled for enemy soldiers who have landed before you. If you spot another soldier, try to veer in another direction and choose an alternate landing spot, since the soldier who already landed (or who will be landing before you) will likely already be armed with a weapon.

Each time your soldier lands on the island at the start of a match, they're equipped only with their Harvesting Tool. This can be used to gather resources (wood, stone, and metal) for building, but it can also be used as a close-range weapon. The problem is, you'll need to whack an enemy with the Harvesting Tool multiple times to do any damage, and this pickaxe is no match against a soldier armed with a gun or explosive weapon. When choosing a landing location, if you know where a chest will likely be found, this is a great place to start building your arsenal.

Displayed below the mini-map on the main game screen is a timer that tells you when the storm will form, or when it will next expand and move. In this case, the storm will expand and move again in two minutes and fifty-two seconds.

Within the mini-map, follow the white line to discover the shortest route between your current location on the island and the next safe zone (which is the area not yet made uninhabitable by the storm).

Based on the situation when you land, first find and grab a weapon (and ammo), and then seek out somewhere to take cover, if necessary, should an enemy spot you and immediately start shooting. If no enemies are in the area, start exploring the island, building up your soldier's arsenal, and choose what type of strategy you plan to adopt in order to survive until the End Game.

Beware of the Deadly Storm

As if dealing with up to 99 enemies on the island wasn't enough, within minutes after your soldier's arrival, a deadly storm will form and begin to expand, until it eventually engulfs almost the entire island, during the final minutes of a match (when only a few soldiers remain alive).

Shown here is the Island Map view of the soldier's current location. In this case, the soldier (who is currently located within Sunny Steps) has just under three minutes to travel a far distance to reach the next safe zone. Since the storm has not yet formed on the island, the next safe zone appears as a large white circle on the Island Map.

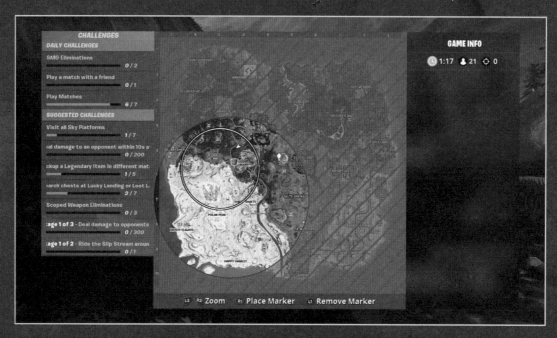

Both within the mini-map, as well as on the Island Map screen, the areas of the island shown in pink have already been made uninhabitable by the storm. Anytime you see two circles displayed on the Island Map, the outer circle is the current safe area, and the inner (smaller) circle shows you where the safe region will be once the deadly storm expands and moves again.

While exploring the island, the edge of the storm is depicted as a blue wall. As long as you stay on the safe side of the blue wall (within the safe zone circle depicted on the map), your biggest concern will be the enemy soldiers remaining on the island who are trying to eliminate your soldier from the match. Shown here on the iPad version of Fortnite: Battle Royale, the soldier is standing on the safe side of the storm's blue wall.

For each second your soldier finds himself on the wrong side of the blue wall and caught within the deadly storm (shown here on an iPad), some of their Health meter will be depleted. Once your soldier's Health meter reaches zero, they will immediately be eliminated from the match. If your soldier enters the storm ravaged area during the early stages of the match, the speed that their Health meter will be depleted starts off slow. Later in the match, your soldier will receive greater damage to their Health meter faster. On most gaming systems a soldier's Health and Shield meters are displayed near the bottom-center of the screen. When playing on an iPad, these meters can be found near the top-left corner of the screen, next to the mini-map.

There will be times when your soldier has to travel a far distance from the currently safe area to what will be the new safe region once the storm expands and moves again. You'll discover it's very difficult (and sometimes impossible) to outrun the storm for an extended amount of time, unless your soldier is riding in a vehicle or utilizing some other mode of transportation on the island (such as a Rift-To-Go, Launch Pad, or Grappler).

Shields do not protect your soldier from damage caused by the storm, or injury incurred as the result of a fall. Shields do, however, offer protection from incoming weapon attacks and explosions.

Especially if you're experiencing a Duos or Squads match, a Quadcrasher is useful because it holds multiple soldiers at once, so one soldier can drive, and the others can use their weapons (or build) while the vehicle is in motion. Of course, a Quadcrasher can also be ridden solo, and it provides a fast way to travel around the island and, if necessary, outrun the storm.

Learn How to Read the Island Map

Driving or riding in a vehicle is the fastest and easiest way to travel around the island and successfully outrun the movement of the storm. A Hoverboard (also referred to as a Driftboard) allows one soldier to travel at high speeds with incredible maneuverability.

This is what the Island Map looked like near the start of Season 9. As you'll discover, with each new gaming season, major geographical changes occur on the island. New points of interest are introduced, while some pre-existing points of interest may be destroyed and removed, or dramatically transformed.

The Island Map screen offers a lot of information at any given time, including:

Some vehicles, like a Baller, are a bit more difficult to maneuver, but offer much better protection against incoming attacks while allowing your soldier to travel at a faster speed than running on foot.

- From the Island Map you can see the random route the bus will travel over the island, while your soldier is in the pre-deployment area or riding on the Battle Bus.

- You're able to clearly see all of the labeled points of interest on the map.
- Your soldier's current location is displayed on the map as a small, arrow-shaped icon. Different colored icons are used to show you the current location of your partner or squad mates if you're playing a Duos, Squads, or a team-oriented match. The location of your enemies is never displayed on the Island Map.
- The pink area on the map is the area of the island that's already been engulfed by the deadly storm and is uninhabitable.
- The outer circle on the map shows the current safe zone, while the inner circle shows where the safe zone will be once the storm expands and moves again.
- Markers can be placed on the map to help you, your partner, or your squad mates navigate to a specific location on the island.

How to Take Advantage of Map Coordinates and Markers

To make finding specific areas on the map easier, use the map coordinates system. Notice that along the top of the Island Map screen are the letters "A" through "J," and along the left edge of the map are the numbers "1" through "10." Anytime you need to identify a location on the map, use its coordinates. For example, during Season 9, Snobby Shores was located at map coordinates A5, and Mega Mall was located at map coordinates H6. Lazy Lagoon could be found near map coordinates F3, and Pleasant Park, for example, was at map coordinates C3.5.

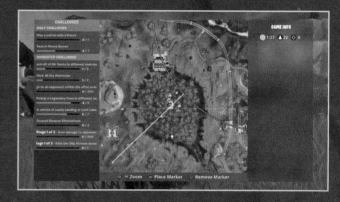

While you're looking at the Island Map, it's possible to zoom in on any location in order to see more detail.

Markers can also be placed on the Island Map. At the start of a match, while you're still in the pre-deployment area, or while riding on the Battle Bus, placing a Marker on the map shows your partner or squad mates where you intend to land, and allows you to quickly set a rendezvous location without having to talk. Using the zoom feature on the Island Map, Fatal Fields is shown here. There's a blue Marker located within this point of interest.

You, as well as your partner or squad mates, can all add different colored Markers to the Island Map screen, as needed.

Once one or more Markers have been placed on the Map Screen, they're displayed as colored flares on the main game screen, and they can be seen from great distances. Even if you're playing a Solo match, and you know you're trying to reach a specific location, placing a Marker on the Island Map makes that location easier to see from a distance when you're navigating your way to it.

Keep in mind, whenever you place a Marker on the Island Map, only you, your partner, and/or your squad mates can see it. Gamers controlling enemy soldiers cannot see your Marker(s). Upon reaching a location that's been marked on the map, the colored flare on the main game screen (and its related Marker on the Island Map) will automatically disappear. As you're approaching a Marker, however, the distance between your soldier's current location and that Marker is displayed on the screen.

Don't Forget to Manage Your Soldier's Arsenal and Inventory

In addition to your soldier's Harvesting Tool (which can also be used as a close-range weapon, although it's not too powerful), every soldier can carry up to six additional weapons or items in their main inventory, as well as certain other types of weapons and items in conjunction with their resources. To access these other items or weapons, you'll need to quickly access the Inventory Management screen or switch from Combat mode to Building mode.

When in Combat mode, your soldier can use any guns or weapons currently in their inventory. Building mode is used to build structures from scratch using any combination of the four different-shaped building tiles that can be created from wood, stone, or metal.

Each of the *Fortnite: Battle Royale* weapons fall into one of the following categories:

Close-Range Weapons—Pistols are an example of a close-range weapon. These are best used when you're fighting within a structure, and you're not too far away from your target. As you get farther away from your target, the weapon will become harder to aim and inflict less damage. Pistols tend to be the weakest guns in the game. When you have the opportunity to switch them out for a more powerful close- to mid-range weapon, do so.

Mid-Range Weapons—These tend to be more versatile than close-range weapons, so they can be used with decent accuracy in a broader range of indoor or outdoor combat scenarios.

Long-Range Weapons—Sniper Rifles with a scope are just one example of a long-range weapon that shoots bullets with extreme accuracy when you're far away from your target. When using any weapon with a scope, if you just point the gun and shoot, you'll experience less accuracy than if you press the Aim button, position your enemy within the targeting crosshairs, and then fire the gun.

Explosive Weapons—As you explore the island, you'll be able to find, grab, store, and then use a variety of different throwable explosive weapons, such as Grenades or Dynamite. These tend to work best when you're mid-range from your opponent, since you don't want your soldier to be too close to the explosion that occurs once any of these weapons detonates.

Explosive Projectile Weapons Launchers— Anytime you need to destroy buildings, structures, or vehicles, for example, as well as the enemies within them, projectile explosive weapons allow you to target enemies from a distance, and then shoot explosive ammo with extreme accuracy. Some of the Projectile Explosive Weapons you may discover on the island include: Rocket Launchers, Guided Missile Launchers, Grenade Launchers, Boom Bows, and/or Quad Launchers. Depending on the gaming season, not all of these weapons will be available all of the time.

A Grenade Launcher allows you to shoot Grenades a lot farther than a handheld Grenade can be thrown. Whether they're shot or thrown, Grenades function the same way. It's best to shoot or toss them through an open door or window so they land inside of a structure before they detonate in order to cause destructive damage. If a Grenade hits a solid wall, it will bounce off of it. Shown here, the soldier is aiming a Grenade Launcher so the Grenade flies into the second-story window of the house.

Traps and Specialty Weapons— During each gaming season, a different selection of Traps and specialty weapons are made available. A Trap, for example, can be placed on any flat surface, such as a floor, ceiling, or wall

of a structure. Depending on the type of Trap being used, an enemy that gets caught in one could be instantly defeated or at least injured. In some cases, Traps have a different impact on the soldier who activates it. In addition to Traps, depending on the gaming season, you may discover specialty weapons, such as Cannons (which can be ridden and shoot destructive cannon balls), or Turrets (which can be mounted in one place and then rain bullets on an enemy target).

Assault Rifles (ARs) are the most versatile weapons, because they're powerful and useful at close-range, mid-range, or even at a distance. Shown here are the stats for an Uncommon Heavy Assault Rifle.

There are several different model Pistols typically available on the island (such as Pistols, Hand Canons, Six Shooters, Suppressed Pistols, Duel Pistols, and Revolvers). These tend to be the weakest type of gun available, and they're best used for close-range fighting (when your soldier is within a building or structure, for example).

Some types of Pistols have higher Damage and DPS ratings, a faster Fire Rate, a larger Magazine Size, and/or faster Reload time than others. The most versatile type of Pistol is a Scoped Revolver. Thanks to its scope, it can be used from any distance. Ideally, you want to find and keep a Legendary Scoped Revolver in your arsenal.

Shotguns are also versatile weapons, since they can cause damage from almost any distance. The trick is to find and grab the best ranked and most powerful Shotgun model you can during a match. Shotguns fire Shells, which burst apart when fired, meaning each shot can inflict damage over a greater area, based on the distance a round travels before impact. When the distance is too far, the Shell fragments disperse over a greater area. This reduces the damage each round causes on its target. Shown here is a Tactical Shotgun, which is typically one of the more common weapons you'll find on the island.

Sniper Rifles are powerful long-range weapons that include a scope. They tend to have a small Magazine size and long reload time, but they're great for achieving headshots from a distance, especially if you catch your enemy off-guard and standing still. The different type of Sniper Rifles are best used during the early-to mid-stages of a match, when enemies can still be far apart. During the End Game, all remaining soldiers are typically very close together, so a Sniper Rifle is often less useful.

Try to find and use a Sniper Rifle with a large Mag Size, so you'll need to reload less frequently during firefights. When using a weapon with a small Mag Size, position your soldier behind a protective barrier when reloading.

One benefit to a Legendary Suppressed Sniper Rifle is that it makes very little noise when fired. This makes it harder for your target(s) to pinpoint the shooter's location when they're far away. If your enemy can't figure out where your soldier is, they can't accurately shoot back.

The drawback to Shotguns is they typically have a small Magazine size, capable of holding just one or two Shells at a time before a reload is needed. These weapons also tend to have a slow reload time. For example, a Legendary Double Barrel Shotgun takes 2.7 seconds to reload, but each direct hit can inflict up to 120 Damage. The Pump Shotgun (shown here) works nicely as a close-range weapon when you're exploring the inside of houses, buildings, or structures, for example.

Submachine Guns (SMGs) *are excellent at close- to mid-range, because they have a very fast Fire Rate and can cause a good amount of damage quickly. Their Magazine Size tends to be rather large (20 rounds or more before a reload is required). The farther you are from your target, however, the worse the aiming accuracy will be when using an SMG.*

Instead of holding down the trigger and utilizing Automatic Firing mode, SMGs tend to be more accurate if you use Burst mode. In other words, press the trigger for a second or two, release, and then press the trigger again, instead of holding it down. A Common Suppressed Submachine Gun is shown here. It's one of several types of SMGs typically available on the island.

Don't forget, within each weapon or gun category, there are multiple types of weapons, and each weapon type is rated based on its color-coded Rarity (Common, Uncommon, Rare, Epic, or Legendary). A weapon's Rarity helps to determine its overall power and capabilities based on criteria such as its Damage Per Second (DPS), overall Damage capabilities, Fire Rate, Magazine Size, and Reload Time.

If you're carrying a specific weapon that you really like, and it's rated as Rare for example, but you're able to find the same weapon, but the new one is ranked as Epic or Legendary, always swap it out for the more powerful version of the weapon, unless you have room in your inventory for both weapons. Later, when you need to get rid of a weapon to make room for something else, drop or swap out the weakest weapon(s) you have.

At any given time, more than 100 different weapon styles and variations are available on the island. With each new game update or gaming season, new weapons are introduced, others are removed altogether, and some have their capabilities tweaked—making them either more powerful or less powerful.

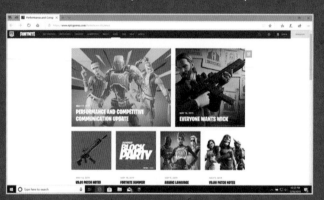

Anytime a new weapon is introduced into Fortnite: Battle Royale, *information about it appears on the Epic games website, within the News section (www.epicgames.com/fortnite/en-US/news).*

You'll also see announcements about new weapons within the News screen that's featured in the game itself. As news gets released, this screen appears when you launch the game. You can view the News screen anytime by accessing the News option from the Game Menu, which was redesigned at the end of a Season 9.

From the News screen within the game, be sure to click on the Patch Notes button to read the latest details about new weapons, features, and functions added to *Fortnite: Battle Royale*.

When a weapon becomes less powerful in *Fortnite: Battle Royale*, it's referred to as having been "nerfed." Anytime a weapon gets removed from the game, this is referred to as being "vaulted," but that same weapon could be re-introduced into the game anytime in the future.

Where to Find Weapons on the Island

The arsenal a soldier carries must be collected and managed by the gamer controlling that soldier. With limited space in a soldier's inventory, it's important to maintain an arsenal that's useful in all types of fighting situations and terrain types.

Opening chests is another way to build your soldier's arsenal, often without the danger of having to fight off enemies.

Supply Drops are rare and randomly drop from the sky. These tend to include powerful and rare weapons. However, to grab them, you must be the first person to arrive at and open the Supply Drop's wooden crate.

Weapons (and ammo) can be found lying on the ground, out in the open. These are often found within buildings or structures, but sometimes outside.

Added to Fortnite: Battle Royale *during Season 9, Loot Carriers work just like Supply Drops, but it's necessary to shoot them out of the sky in order to collect the random selection of weapons and loot items being carried within them. These Loot Carriers are drones that fly overhead randomly during matches, so keep your eyes peeled!*

On the Island Map, points of interest that are labeled in yellow indicate where you're most apt to find Loot Carriers randomly flying around. When on the island, you'll see these drones flying at all altitudes–some are high up (shown here) and require a gun to shoot them down. Some Loot Carriers, however, hover closer to the ground and can be destroyed using your soldier's Harvesting Tool.

Each Vending Machine offers a different inventory selection. Approach the Vending Machine and watch for the available items to be displayed. When an item appears that you want, press the Select button on your keyboard or controller.

A Loot Llama looks like a colorful piñata. They get randomly scattered throughout the island but are much rarer than chests. They also tend to contain a larger and more powerful selection of weapons, ammo, and loot items.

Especially during the mid- to final stages of a match, one of the best ways to quickly and dramatically improve your soldier's arsenal is to fight and defeat enemy soldiers. As soon as a soldier is defeated, not only are they removed from the match instantly, but everything the deceased soldier was carrying falls to the ground and can be grabbed by any of the surviving soldiers. Even if you don't defeat an enemy, you can still grab what a fallen enemy leaves behind after they've lost a firefight against someone else. Through the scope, you can see the weapons, ammo, and loot items left behind by a soldier who didn't survive.

Vending Machines are also a great source for acquiring powerful weapons during a match. These too are randomly scattered throughout the island.

Managing Your Soldier's Inventory

At any time during a match, an overview of your soldier's inventory is displayed on the screen. Depending on which gaming system you're using, this information is typically found near the bottom-right corner.

In addition to your soldier's Harvesting Tool, which he or she always carries and cannot drop at any time, your soldier has six Inventory Slots that can hold weapons or certain types of loot items (such as Health and Shield replenishment items).

As you're looking at the inventory icons displayed in the bottom-right corner of the screen, the number associated with each item tells you one of two things. If the icon relates to a weapon, it shows you how much compatible ammo you currently have for that weapon. If the icon is for an item, it shows you how many of that item you have on hand. The weapon or item that's currently selected and active will display a yellow box around its inventory icon slot.

To see and manage your soldier's entire inventory, it's necessary to access their Inventory screen. This is done by pressing the assigned Inventory button on your keyboard/mouse or controller.

The Inventory Management screen displays a lot of useful information. On the top-right side of the screen, you'll see a summary of the Resources your soldier is carrying –including wood, stone, and metal. Below this, also on the right side of the screen, is a summary of the ammunition your soldier currently has on hand. Each ammo icon represents one of the five types of ammo (Light Bullets, Medium Bullets, Heavy Bullets, Shells, and Rockets), and shows how many rounds of each ammo type you have available.

Displayed to the right of your soldier's Resources on the Inventory screen (when applicable) is information about the Traps and other items (such as Cozy Campfires), that are stored in your soldier's inventory, but that don't take up one of the six main Inventory Slots. To access any of these items, while viewing the main game screen, switch to Building mode using the assigned keyboard/ mouse key or controller button, and then press the keyboard key, mouse button, or controller button assigned to the additional weapons and tools.

When your soldier is holding multiple Traps or items that are not included within the six main Inventory Slots (when playing on a console-based gaming system), you'll need to enter into Building mode, and then keep pressing the appropriate controller button to scroll through the items in order to select the one you want to use. On a computer, each item is bound to a different keyboard key or mouse button.

Displayed in the bottom-right corner of the Inventory screen are the soldier's Inventory Slots. The left-most slot (on most gaming systems) always holds the Harvesting Tool. However, it's possible to rearrange the items being held in the other six slots to make them easier to access during a match.

As you're looking at the Inventory screen, use the directional controls to highlight and select the weapon, ammo type, or item you want to access or use. The selected item's icon will display a yellow frame around it.

If you have a weapon selected, details about the weapon's category, color-coded rarity, and stats are displayed on the left side of the screen. When you're not sure how to best use a weapon or what type of ammo it requires, for example, this is a quick way to access the information.

Anytime you access your soldier's Inventory screen, this takes your attention away from the main game screen and what's happening on the island. The match does not pause, so your soldier potentially becomes vulnerable to attack.

Only access the Inventory screen when you're in a safe location (such as small and enclosed room with the door shut). While viewing this screen, even though you can't see what's happening around your soldier, you can still hear sound effects, so pay attention to the sound of approaching enemies or nearby weapons firing. If it sounds like an enemy is approaching or you may soon be under attack, exit from the Inventory screen quickly and be ready to take defensive actions!

How to Rearrange What's in Inventory Slots

Whenever you pick up a new weapon or loot item, it automatically gets placed within an available Inventory Slot. Your soldier's Inventory Slots initially fill up from left to right.

However, during a match, it's a good strategy to rearrange the items in your inventory so your most powerful and frequently used weapons and items are placed in the left-most slots. To rearrange what's in your Inventory slots, follow these steps:

1. Access your soldier's Inventory screen.
2. Highlight and select one of the items you want to move.
3. On a PC, drag the item from one Inventory slot to another. On a console-based system, select the Move command, and then position the cursor over the slot you want to move the selected item to.

Experienced gamers tend to place their favorite weapon in the left-most Inventory Slot, and then their Health/Shield replenishment item(s) in the right-most slots. Throwable weapons (when available) get placed in the middle Inventory Slots. This strategy, however, is a matter of personal preference.

How to Drop and Share Weapons, Ammo, and Items

If your soldier's six Inventory Slots are filled up, but you find a new weapon or item you want to grab, it becomes necessary to give something up. First choose which item you want to get rid of and select it. Next, face the item you want to pick up and grab it. The item you're holding (the one you want to trade out) will be dropped, making room for the new item you want to grab.

There will be times when you might just want to drop a weapon or item that you no longer want or it's something that you want to share with a partner or squad mate who is standing close to your soldier. To do this, access the Inventory screen, select the item you want to drop, and then press the keyboard key, mouse button, or controller button that's associated with the Drop command. Shown here, a Small Shield Potion was shared between two squad mates.

As you can see here, one squad mate shared a Legendary Hand Cannon with their ally.

If you want to share an item from your inventory and your soldier is currently carrying multiples of that item, select the item you want to share with a nearby ally, and select the Drop command (see in the bottom-right corner of the screen).

From the Drop Items pop-up window, choose how many of that item you want to drop (share). Press the Drop button to drop that amount of the item. Press the Max button to drop the entire inventory of that item your soldier is carrying.

Instead of wasting valuable time using the Drop Items slider, after selecting an item from the Inventory screen, select the Split command to instantly drop half of the quantity of the item that's selected. So if you have six Heavy Bullets for example, and you use the Split command, you'll keep three Heavy Bullets in your inventory and drop three for someone else to pick up.

Anytime you opt to Drop or Share a weapon or item, make sure an ally is nearby and picks it up. Otherwise, any soldier (including your enemies) could stumble upon what you've dropped and grab it. Sometimes, in order to pick up a more powerful or useful item, you'll need to drop a less powerful or less useful item. However, you run the risk of an enemy acquiring it.

How to Accurately Aim and Fire Different Types of Weapons

Depending on the weapon, there are several ways to aim and then fire it. When any gun is active, point it toward your enemy and pull the trigger to fire it. This strategy works well when you're in close range, when time is more important than aiming accuracy because you're close to the enemy and it'll be difficult to miss your intended target. This is referred to as "shooting from the hip."

By pressing the Aim button before pulling the trigger (shown here using a Rare Assault Rifle), you'll achieve more accurate aim for the weapon you're using, particularly if your soldier is crouching and still or standing still. Notice how small the targeting crosshair is that's displayed on the white wall. You can barely make out the white "+". When you press the Aim button, the viewing perspective changes. You'll see your target from the end of a gun's barrel, and the target will appear closer.

Shown here, the soldier is running toward the building and is ready to fire her weapon. Notice the white aiming crosshairs (seen on the wall of the building) are very large. If he were to fire, the bullet would hit somewhere within this large crosshair area.

Simply by standing still, the targeting crosshairs for the weapon shrinks a lot, meaning that he'll be able to aim more accurately. To achieve the most precise aim, pressing the Aim button before pulling the trigger works best, but this takes slightly longer. If there were an enemy standing in front of him at close range, the fraction of a second it takes to press the Aim button could give the enemy the time needed to shoot their own weapon first.

Anytime you're using a weapon with a built-in scope, pressing the Aim button activates the scope and changes your view. The farther you are from your target, the more you may need to compensate for bullet drop, so aim slightly higher than your intended target. Learning to accurately account for bullet drop takes practice, and the technique varies for each type of long-range weapon.

Whenever you point an active weapon at any target, you'll see its targeting crosshairs. The smaller the crosshairs appear, the more accurate your shot will be. Standing still and crouching will reduce the size of the crosshairs, while walking, running, or jumping will increase the size of the crosshairs and greatly reduce your aiming accuracy.

The aiming process for throwable weapons (various types of Grenades) is different than shooting a gun. Notice the targeting crosshairs look different. When you toss a Grenade, it follows an arc-like trajectory. As you're aiming the Grenade, you'll see an outline for the trajectory for that weapon. In some cases, if you're trying to toss a Grenade through a small open window of a building or fortress, it may be necessary to aim slightly higher than your intended target.

As soon as a soldier's Health meter hits zero, they're immediately eliminated from the match. Remember, if you're playing a Duos, Squads, or 50v50 (Team Rumble) match, for example, an ally has 90 seconds to grab your soldier's Reboot Card and return it to a Respawn Van, which allows the eliminated soldier to be returned to a match. Successfully reaching a Respawn Van can be a challenge if it's being guarded by enemies.

Pay Attention to Your Soldier's Health and Shield Meters

Displayed near the bottom-center of the screen on most gaming systems are your soldier's Health and Shield meters.

Initially when a match kicks off, a soldier's Shields meter is at zero. To activate your soldier's Shields, use any Shield replenishment item, such as a Small Shield Potion, Shield Potion (shown here), Chug Jug, or Mushrooms. Once activated, Shields will protect your soldier against incoming gun fire and explosions, but not against falls or damage caused by the storm. If your soldier is hit by incoming gunfire or an explosion, for example, first their Shield meter will get depleted, followed by their Health meter. Items, like a Shield Potion, can be found, collected, stored in your soldier's inventory, and then used as needed. Other items, like Mushrooms, need to be consumed where they're found.

At the start of a match, your soldier's Health meter will be at 100 percent. Each time they receive injury as a result of an attack, fall, getting caught in an explosion, or wind up within the storm, for example, some (or in some cases all) of their Health gets depleted.

Fortnite: Battle Royale Is Constantly Evolving

Once you begin playing *Fortnite: Battle Royale*, you'll notice that every week, Epic Games releases a new update or patch, and that one or more new weapons and/or loot items are introduced. At the same time, some items may get "vaulted" (temporarily or permanently removed from the game). You may also discover alterations to the Island Map, as new points of interest are introduced, or pre-existing locations get modified or removed.

To stay up-to-date on all of the weapons currently available within *Fortnite: Battle Royale*, and to see the ratings for each weapon, check out any of these independent websites:

- **Fortnite Weapon Stats & Info**—https://fortnitestats.com/weapons
- **Gamepedia Fortnite Wiki**—https://fortnite.gamepedia.com/Fortnite_Wiki
- **GameSkinny Fortnite Weapons List**—www.gameskinny.com/9mt22/complete-fortnite-battle-royale-weapons-stats-list
- **Metabomb**—www.metabomb.net/fortnite-battle-royale/gameplay-guides/fortnite-battle-royale-all-weapons-tier-list-with-stats-14
- **Tracker Network (Fortnite)**—https://db.fortnitetracker.com/weapons

You can expect subtle as well as major geographic changes to occur on the island on a pretty regular basis; as well as for new (temporary) game play modes to be introduced; and for new outfits and items to be released on a daily basis within the Item Shop.

Practice Your Building Skills

Building continues to be an important skill that's typically required to achieve #1 Victory Royale during a match. Strategies for improving your building skills will be covered in the next section. When it comes to building, your speed is as important as what you build.

Using wood, stone, and metal resources that your soldier harvests using the Harvesting Tool, or collects during a match, he or she is able to build protective barriers, structures, ramps, bridges, and even elaborate fortresses. Shown here, wood is being harvested from trees using the soldier's Harvesting tool. To harvest wood, smash anything made of wood that you encounter on the island, including trees, some walls, wooden structures, or furniture.

Look for resource icons and grab them. Shown here is a Stone resource icon. As you can see, there's a small yellow and black banner that's within the banner describing the item. This particular resource icon is worth 30 Stone. Finding and grabbing these resource icons allows you to collect bundles of wood, stone, or metal that immediately get added to your soldier's inventory.

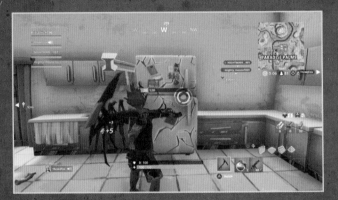

To harvest stone, use the Harvesting Tool to smash anything made of stone that you find on the island, such as rock piles, brick walls, or any structures made from stone.

Metal is the strongest material to build with. To harvest metal, smash anything made of metal that you come across while exploring the island, such as disabled vehicles, metal structures, or metal equipment (including appliances within a home).

Welcome to the Mysterious Island!

One skill you'll need to master is safely traveling around the island to get from place to place and/or explore. Shown here, a soldier is traveling through a network of Slipstreams that were introduced into the game at the start of Season 9.

Do you have what it takes to survive, or will you quickly be defeated by one of the other soldiers on the island? To consistently defeat your enemies in firefights and win #1 Victory Royale, you'll need to master the art of survival, be able to build quickly, avoid the deadly storm, and learn how to use the many guns and explosive weapons at your disposal.

However, when it comes to working with weapons during a match, you'll consistently need to use six essential skills, including:

1. Finding weapons and then adding the best selection of them to your soldier's arsenal. The weapons you collect get stored within your soldier's backpack. It only has slots for up to six weapons and/or loot items (excluding your soldier's Harvesting Tool, which can also be used as a short-range weapon).

2. Choosing the most appropriate weapon based on each combat situation. This means quickly analyzing the challenges and rivals you're currently facing, and

*In order to build, a soldier needs to switch from **Combat** mode to **Building** mode. While in **Building** mode, they're unable to use any weapons. Based on what resources your soldier has on hand, choose the best one to build with, and then mix and match the four different-shaped building tiles available to construct whatever you need, where you need it.*

selecting a close-range, mid-range, or long-range gun, an explosive weapon, or a projectile explosive weapon that'll help you get the current job done.

3. Collecting and stockpiling the different types of ammunition and making sure you have an ample supply of ammunition for each weapon you want to use.

4. Positioning yourself in the ideal location, with direct line-of-sight to your target(s), so you can inflict damage in the most accurate and efficient way possible. Headshots always cause more damage than a body shot, for example, when targeting enemies.

5. Aiming each type of weapon, so you're able to consistently hit your targets, without wasting ammunition or increasing the risk of your enemies having time to shoot back. When your soldier crouches down while shooting a weapon, their aim will always improve.

6. Shooting the active weapon your soldier is holding, and then quickly switching between weapons as needed.

You'll also need to take cover each time a weapon needs to be reloaded.

Once you get good at performing each of these tasks, it'll still take a lot of practice to become a highly skilled sharpshooter who is capable of using single shots to defeat enemies. Plus, you'll need to discover how to best use the weapons at your disposal to destroy structures and fortresses in which your enemies may be hiding.

By the way, if you notice that the game gets sluggish or stutters while you're playing, this often has to do with the speed of your Internet connection. Try using a direct (cabled) connection between your gaming system and the Internet's modem/router, as opposed to a wireless Wi-Fi connection. Having a high-speed Internet connection improves the overall performance of the game.

The next section of this unofficial strategy guide is chock full of game play tips and strategies that'll help you master various aspects of *Fortnite: Battle Royale*. Learning these strategies, combined with plenty of practice, will help you stay alive longer and defeat more enemies during each match.

SECTION 3

101 EXTREME SURVIVAL TECHNIQUES

473

2,600

GEAR   OUTFIT

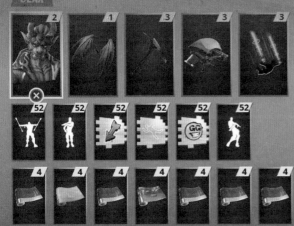

RARE | OUTFIT
FIREWALKER

No matter what gaming season you're about to experience, the 101 tips and strategies offered in this section will help you get the most out of your *Fortnite: Battle Royale* gaming experience. These tips are divided into a dozen sections for easy reference. Remember, since every match will be totally different from the last, you'll need to pick and choose which strategies to implement, based on your location on the island and the challenges you're facing at any given moment.

Customizing Your Soldier

By visiting the Locker before a match, you're able to customize the appearance of your soldier using outfits and items that you've previously purchased and/or unlocked.

#1—Avoid Brightly Colored Outfits

Depending on the climate of the area of the island you're exploring, you might be surrounded by dense forest, snow and ice covered terrain, water, desert, or lush green areas, for

example. When your soldier is dressed in a brightly colored outfit, they'll stand out and be easier to spot, especially when they're out in the open.

Consider choosing an outfit with darker or camouflage coloring to help your soldier blend in better with their surroundings, especially when they're hiding behind an object.

The "hit box" for all of the outfits available in Fortnite: Battle Royale *is exactly the same, so having your soldier wear an outfit that makes them appear larger does not make them easier to target and accurately shoot at during combat. All the outfits are for cosmetic purposes only and offer no shielding, defensive, or tactical advantage whatsoever, except that brightly colored outfits are often easier for other gamers to spot.*

By combining an outfit with a Harvesting Tool design and Back Bling design that come from different sets, for example, you're able to make your soldier look unique. It's up to you whether you want your soldier to appear scary, intimidating, tough, whimsical, or outrageous looking.

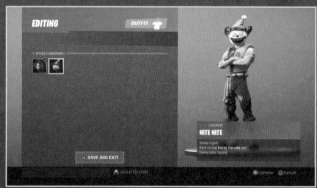

Keep in mind, a growing number of outfits offer unlockable Styles, which allow you to further customize your soldier's appearance. Styles typically need to be unlocked by completing Style-based challenges once an outfit has been acquired. Shown here are two different Styles associated with an outfit called Nite Nite.

#2—All Glider Designs Function the Same

Most optional outfits or sets offered within Fortnite: Battle Royale *include a unique-looking Glider design. While each design looks totally different, they all function exactly the same way. None offers an advantage over another.*

The first time you'll use a Glider is at the start of a match, once your soldier leaps from the Battle Bus. Just before reaching land, the Glider will automatically deploy to ensure a safe landing. At any time during the freefall, slow down your soldier's descent and improve your navigational control by manually activating your soldier's Glider. By slowing down how fast your soldier falls, you have the ability to glide through the air longer and travel a farther distance. In fact, with careful navigation, you should be able to cross almost half of the island during freefall by deploying the Glider early on.

During a match, there will be instances when you'll be able to deploy your soldier's Glider to travel from one location of the island to another, or to quickly escape from one high-up area to a lower-down area. One way to do this is to collect and then later use the Glider item. Once this item is in your inventory, you can deploy it 10 times. Keep in mind, perfect timing is essential when leaping off of a mountain, cliff, tall building, or large structure. If you deploy the Glider too late, your soldier will crash to the ground. This will result in a severe injury (or worse).

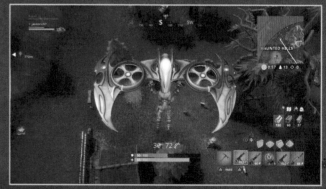

Placing and then stepping onto a Launch Pad (shown here), Bounce Pad, using a Rift-To-Go, or stepping through a Rift are other ways for your soldier to go airborne and then need to deploy their Glider to achieve a safe landing. During a match, enemy soldiers can (and will) shoot at your soldier while they're airborne and using their Glider. You can also shoot at enemies as they travel via their own Glider. A direct hit with a Rocket Launcher will cause the most damage, but multiple direct bullet hits will do the trick as well when it comes to defeating airborne enemies.

While a Launch Pad takes a few seconds to set up, a Rift-To-Go can be found, collected, stored in your soldier's inventory, and then activated exactly when and where it's needed if your soldier wants to go airborne.

#3—Use Emotes Wisely

Fortnite: Battle Royale *offers several types of emotes, and then hundreds of variations of each emote type. While these are fun to use and allow you to show off your personality as you taunt your enemies, don't let using emotes distract you. To use one of the six emotes you've previously selected, access the Emotes menu, or press the keyboard key assigned to a specific emote. When you do this, your view of the game screen will change momentarily, which could provide an enemy with an opportunity to sneak up and launch a surprise attack.*

Only use emotes when you're sure it's safe to do so, such as when you're in a remote area and you've just defeated an enemy. The gamer you've just eliminated from the match will be able to see your victory dance if you choose to showcase a Dance Move.

Many gamers like to showcase their Dance Moves while in the pre-deployment area, but this type of emote can also be used to taunt enemies, attract attention, distract enemies, or gloat after a victory. Here, the soldier is using the attention-grabbing Fire Spinner Dance Move (emote) as he rides a Hoverboard through the streets of Neo Tilted. This is a sure way to capture the attention of enemies and invite them to start shooting!

After you've taken over an enemy's fortress or encampment, for example, you can decorate any flat surface on the inside or outside of that structure using one or more Spray Paint Tags.

One type of emote offered in the game are toys, such as a basketball. You can carry this around as one of your six emotes, and then when you discover a basketball court, for example, take a few moments to play hoops. Keep in mind, while you do this, an enemy soldier could sneak up and launch an attack or shoot at you from a distance (using a weapon with a scope).

#4—Upgrade Your Battle Pass

At the start of any new gaming season, Epic Games offers a new Battle Pass that must be purchased. A basic Battle Pass gives you the opportunity to complete 100 Tiers worth of challenges, and for each one you complete, you unlock a prize. A typical Battle Pass includes at least four exclusive outfits that can be unlocked, as well as a selection of Harvesting Tool designs, Glider designs, Contrail designs, and emotes that can be unlocked one at a time. These items are only available from the Battle Pass and will no longer be available once the gaming season associated with that Battle Pass ends.

Instead of purchasing a basic Battle Pass (for 950 V-Bucks, which is equivalent to about $9.50 US), it's possible to upgrade your purchase to a Royale Bundle Battle Pass (for 2,800 V-Bucks, which is equivalent to about $28.00 US). This allows you to instantly unlock the first 25 Battle Pass Tiers and acquire the prizes associated with those Tiers without having to complete any challenges.

By purchasing a Royale Bundle Battle Pass, you're typically able to unlock at least two exclusive and limited-edition outfits immediately, which you can use to customize the appearance of your soldier.

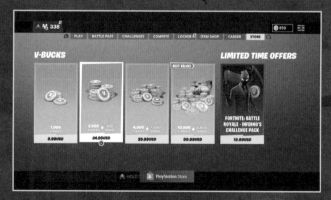

Also available at least once or twice per gaming season, a special Bundle Package can be purchased from the Store, as opposed to the Item Shop. These Bundles typically cost either $4.99 or $9.99, and include a limited-edition outfit, other exclusive items used to customize your soldier's appearance, plus a bundle of V-Bucks.

#5—Adjust Your Gaming Controls

Before any match, from the Lobby, you have the option to access the Settings menu to customize the controller (or keyboard/mouse) options that'll impact your ability to control your soldier and the responsiveness of the controls you're using. To access the Settings menu, select the menu icon that's displayed in the top-right corner of the screen on most gaming systems. It looks like three horizontal lines, and then select the gear-shaped Settings menu icon.

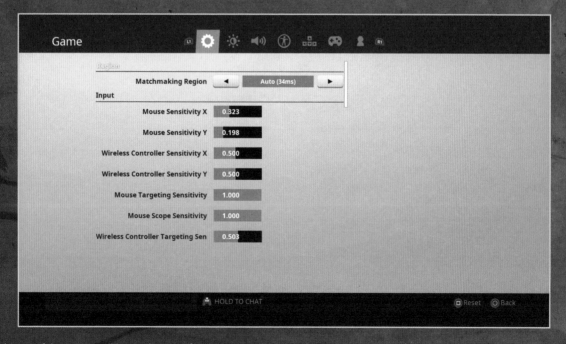

Along the top of the screen will be a selection of menu icons, which vary based on the gaming system you're using. On the PS4, for example, the menu icons include (from left to right): Game (shown here), Brightness, Audio, Accessibility, Input, Wireless Controller, and Account.

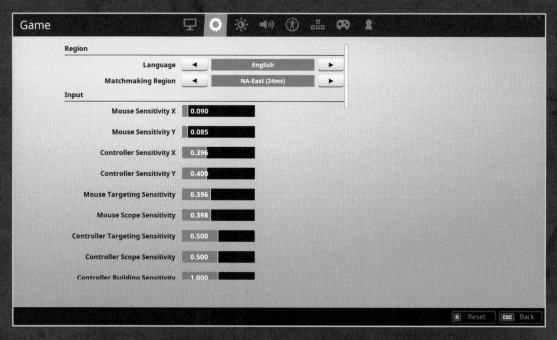

Video					
Window Mode	◄	Fullscreen		►	
Display Resolution	◄	1920x1080 16:9		►	
Frame Rate Limit	◄	Unlimited		►	
Quality	LOW	MEDIUM	HIGH	EPIC	AUTO
3D Resolution	1920 x 1080 (100.0%)				
View Distance	NEAR	MEDIUM	FAR	EPIC	
Shadows	OFF	MEDIUM	HIGH	EPIC	
Anti-Aliasing	OFF	MEDIUM	HIGH	EPIC	
Textures	LOW	MEDIUM	HIGH	EPIC	
Effects	LOW	MEDIUM	HIGH	EPIC	
Post Processing	LOW	MEDIUM	HIGH	EPIC	
Vsync	◄	Off		►	
Motion Blur	◄	On		►	
Show FPS	◄	Off		►	
Allow Multithreaded Rendering	◄	On		►	

ESC Back

When playing the PC version of Fortnite: Battle Royale, *the menu icons include (from left to right): Video, Game, Brightness, Audio, Accessibility, Input, Controller, and Account. From the PC version of* Fortnite: Battle Royale, *make sure you tweak the menu options found within the Video menu, based on your gaming hardware. If you're playing on an older computer containing a slower processor that does not have a state-of-the-art video (graphics) card, you'll need to reduce the display resolution settings and graphic quality in order to ensure the game runs at the proper speed. Allow the game to auto-adjust these settings initially, and then tweak them as needed to enhance your game play experience.*

Game			
Region			
Language	◄	English	►
Matchmaking Region	◄	NA-East (24ms)	►
Input			
Mouse Sensitivity X	0.090		
Mouse Sensitivity Y	0.085		
Controller Sensitivity X	0.396		
Controller Sensitivity Y	0.400		
Mouse Targeting Sensitivity	0.396		
Mouse Scope Sensitivity	0.398		
Controller Targeting Sensitivity	0.500		
Controller Scope Sensitivity	0.500		
Controller Building Sensitivity	1.000		

R Reset   ESC Back

From the Game menu (shown here on a PC), one at a time, adjust the options below the Input heading to a level that matches your gaming skills, style, and personal preference. Whether you're using a controller or a keyboard/mouse to control your soldier within the game, you want to maximize accuracy, responsiveness, and control at all times, as well as achieve the best aiming accuracy possible using your gaming equipment.

Adjust one option at a time by making small changes. Test out the changes by playing one or two matches, or by spending time in the Playground game play mode, and then make additional changes as you deem necessary. Do not just copy the game settings of pro *Fortnite: Battle Royale* gamers.

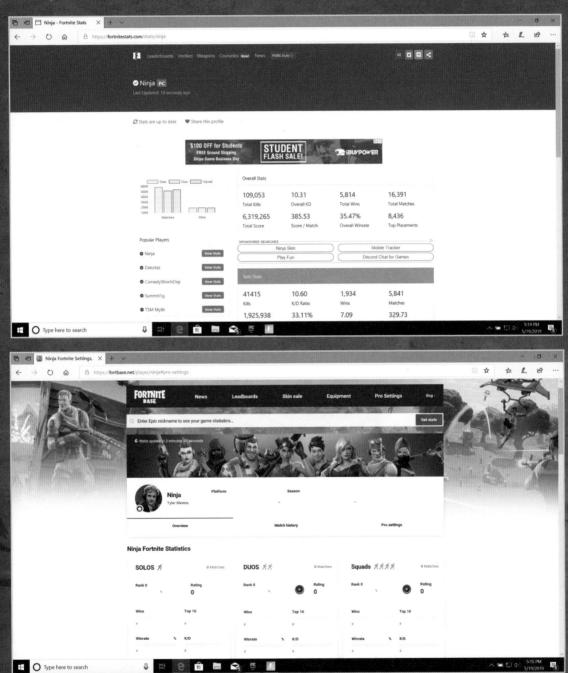

Many websites, such as the free and independent Fortnite Stats & Leaderboard (https://fortnitestats.com) and Fortnite Base (https://fortbase.net/pro-players), publish the customized game settings and the equipment used by top-ranked Fortnite: Battle Royale *players. Knowing what equipment another gamer is using and being able to see their game-related settings is great for reference. However, copying another gamer's settings could actually be detrimental to your gaming success.*

Another gamer's settings are based on their own gaming skill and style, as well as the specific gaming equipment they're using. If your gaming style or skill level is different, or you're using different gaming equipment, the game will react differently. It's important that your game settings be customized specifically for you.

To discover the gaming equipment and customized settings used by top-ranked and pro *Fortnite: Battle Royale* gamers, check out these websites:

- **Best Fortnite Settings**—https://bestfortnitesettings.com/best-fortnite-pro-settings
- **Fortnite Base**—https://fortbase.net/pro-players
- **Fortnite Pro Settings & Config**—https://fortniteconfig.com
- **GamingScan**—www.gamingscan.com/fortnite-competitive-settings-gear
- **ProNettings.net**—https://prosettings.net/best-fortnite-settings-list

If you're using a controller to control your soldier, access the Controller menu to choose between the Old School, Quick Builder, Combat Pro, Builder Pro, or Custom controller layout. Which you should choose is a matter of personal preference, based on your skill level and gaming style. Experiment with each layout and choose the one you're most comfortable with and that gives you quick access to the gaming features and functions that are most important to you during a match.

Whenever you're playing *Fortnite: Battle Royale* on a PS4, Xbox One, or Nintendo Switch console-based gaming system, the default option is to use the controller that came with your gaming system. You always have the option to either replace your controller with one designed for pro gamers, or to connect a keyboard/mouse combo to your gaming system. Many gamers achieve faster response time and better aiming/shooting accuracy when using a keyboard/mouse to control their soldier, as opposed to a controller.

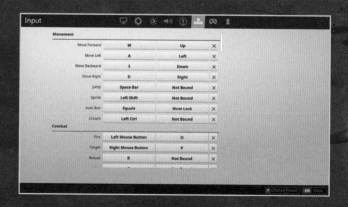

Perhaps the biggest perk of using a keyboard/mouse combo to control the action in Fortnite: Battle Royale *is that you're able to customize all of the key bindings. Access the Input menu (shown here on a PC) to customize which keyboard key or mouse button gets associated with each gaming feature, function, or command based on your personal gaming style.*

#6—Always Listen Carefully to the Game's Sound Effects

During every match, sound effects play an essential role in *Fortnite: Battle Royale.* You can often hear danger approaching before you can see the threat. When playing the Solo game play mode, use high-quality headphones to ensure you can clearly hear every sound effect in the game—from enemy footsteps, to the sounds of doors opening or closing, or the rev of a vehicle's engine. Likewise, when your soldier is in close proximity to a chest, you'll hear a unique sound. You'll also hear the sound of the storm as it approaches.

Anytime you're playing a Duos or Squads match, or any game play mode that requires you to communicate with your allies, definitely consider connecting an optional gaming headset to your gaming system. Gaming headsets allow you to hear the stereo sound effects and music within the game, plus use the headset's built-in microphone to speak with your partner or squad mates during a match. Being able to talk to your allies allows you to plan attacks, coordinate your defense, and approach all in-game challenges in a unified way.

Audio

Volumes

Music Volume 0.46
SoundFX Volume 1.00
Voice Chat Volume 1.00
Cinematics Volume 1.00

Music Volume
Adjusts the volume of music.

Toggles

Subtitles ◄ On ►
Voice Chat ◄ On ►
Push To Talk ◄ Off ►
Voice Channel (Filled Matches) ◄ Party ►
Voice Chat Notifications ◄ On ►

HOLD TO CHAT   Reset   Back

Prior to a match, access the game's Settings menu and then customize the options offered by the Audio sub-menu to ensure the game's sound-related options are adjusted in a way that'll help you focus on the sound effects, while eliminating other audio distractions. Many gamers opt to turn off the game's music altogether by setting the Music Volume option to zero. At the same time, they boost the game's SoundFX Volume to its maximum level. If you're using a gaming headset with a built-in microphone, also adjust the Voice Chat Volume option to a level that allows you to hear your fellow gamers, but that does not drown out the game's sound effects.

Choosing a Landing Spot

At the start of every match, one of the first decisions you'll need to make is when and where your soldier should leap from the Battle Bus in order to begin their descent toward the island.

#7—Pay Attention to When Your Enemies Leap from the Bus

While your soldier is riding in the Battle Bus over the island, adjust the controls so you're able to view the back of the bus. This allows you to see when the 99 other soldiers exit the bus and begin their freefall toward land. If you don't yet have a landing location selected, wait until you see no other enemies leaping from the bus before you have your soldier jump. This helps to ensure they'll land in spot that won't have a bunch of enemies waiting to engage in battle right away.

#8—Look at the Island Map When Choosing a Landing Spot

While in the pre-deployment area before a match, or while riding on the Battle Bus at the start of a match, you're able to switch to the Island Map and see the random route the Battle Bus will travel over the island. This is indicated by a line comprised of arrow-shaped icons.

The route and direction the Battle Bus travels at the start of each match is random. In general, the most popular landing spots are the points of interest located near the very beginning or end of the route that the Battle Bus follows at the start of a specific match.

In this case, at the start of the route, the bus passes over Snobby Shores, and then ends near Lonely Lodge.

Any locations that appear near the center of the island also tend to be popular landing spots. In general, by landing near the center of the island, you'll have less traveling to do once the storm forms and begins to expand and move, so you can focus your attention on other tasks, such as gathering resources, building your soldier's arsenal, or defeating enemies.

New points of interest that have recently been added to the island, or that have been updated or modified recently, also tend to be extremely popular landing spots. At the start of Season 9, for example, Neo Tilted, Pressure Plant, and the redesigned version of Loot Lake were the newest points of interest, or places on the island that changed the most. Gamers are often excited to explore the newest and most popular locations.

#9—Think Strategy Before You Land

By choosing a popular landing spot at the start of a match, you're virtually guaranteed to encounter enemies within moments after landing. This gives you very little time to land, find and grab a weapon (with ammo), and then position your soldier in the best place to defend themselves.

Unless you know there will be weapons to grab right near where you land, be very careful about landing in a spot where enemies have already beaten you there, or you'll be defeated within seconds of landing.

#10—Expect Enemies in Popular Points of Interest

Anytime you land within a popular point of interest, it's important to know exactly where you need to land in order to grab weapons (and ammo), and also be the first soldier to reach that location. When an enemy is able to beat you to the chosen landing spot, they'll grab a weapon and target your soldier the moment they land, while they're still unarmed. (In this case, the soldier has landed on a rooftop in Neo Tilted.)

During the final few moments of freefall, scan the area for weapons to grab, as well as the movement of enemies. If you see an enemy has already landed at your chosen landing spot, veer away quickly and find a safer place to land.

Remember, upon landing on the island, your soldier is equipped only with their Harvesting Tool. This can be used as a close-range weapon, but it requires several direct hits to cause any significant damage to an enemy. Your soldier's Harvesting Tool is no match against any type of gun or explosive weapon.

When landing in a popular point of interest, try to find a landing spot that's as high up as possible (such as the roof of a building or structure or the top of a mountain). Not only will this give you a valuable height advantage over your enemies, it'll also provide a better all-around view of the landing area.

If you land on the roof of a building or house and don't find anything useful outside (on the roof), smash through the roof with your Harvesting Tool to land on the top floor of the building or structure. You'll often encounter weapons lying on the ground or a chest right away. As you're landing, however, if you see an enemy solider already on the roof you intend to land on, seek out another roof.

Once you've landed in a popular point of interest, your two initial goals are to grab a weapon and take cover. Then, once you're momentarily safe, figure out where you want to go and what your next immediate objectives will be. For example, if near your landing spot you're able to grab a weapon and a Shield power-up item, you might want to quickly use the Shield item once you're in a safe location, to activate your soldier's Shields.

#11—Consider Landing in the Outskirts of a Popular Point of Interest

Instead of choosing to land in the heart of a popular point of interest, where you're virtually guaranteed to encounter enemies right away and be forced into combat, consider

landing in the outskirts of a point on interest, preferably on a high-up location. This gives you a few extra moments to find and grab weapons, increase your overall arsenal, scan the area for enemies, and then choose the safest approach into that point of interest.

By landing in the outskirts of a point of interest, you're much less likely to encounter enemies right away. Plus, you'll typically be able to find and grab at least one weapon immediately, especially if you know where to look based on past visits to that location.

This hut is located on a hill just outside of Neo Tilted. It often contains a chest, or at least one weapon (with ammo) lying on the ground.

Once your soldier is armed, travel into the nearby point of interest. You'll be much better prepared to confront the dangers that await.

As you're exploring the outskirts of Neo Tilted, for example, additional weapons, and sometimes a drivable vehicle, can sometimes be found near the hut, surrounding an RV (and/or a car with a trailer).

Just about every point of interest on the island has at least one or two areas located in the outskirts that make for a safer landing spot. Keep in mind, the longer you wait to enter into a popular point of interest, the more likely it'll be that the loot in that area will be snatched up by your enemies before you get there.

On the plus side, when you defeat enemies upon your arrival into that point of interest, you'll be able to collect more weapons, ammo, and items from those defeated soldiers. Plus, there will be fewer enemies remaining in that area, since those who initially landed there will likely fight amongst themselves, causing some to be eliminated from the match.

Choose a landing spot that is just outside of a popular point of interest, collect weapons first, and then target enemies from a distance, assuming your soldier now has a mid-to-long range weapon at their disposal.

#12—Consider Landing in a Remote Location

Located around the outskirts of the island, as well as in between popular points of interest, are many potential landing spots that are remote. Many of these locations offer a nice selection of weapons, ammo, and loot items to find and grab. By choosing one of these remote spots, you'll likely encounter few (or often no) enemies right away, which gives you plenty of extra time to explore and build up a powerful arsenal before your soldier is forced into combat.

By exploring this one outpost, located at the very edge of the island (between map coordinates F1.5 and G1.5), this soldier was able to fill up their arsenal with a selection of weapons, plus collect both Health and Shield-related items.

You'll discover that the island map now is more densely populated with labeled points of interest than ever before. These locations are also located closer together and are often connected by a network of paved roads or clearly defined paths. However, following these roads or paths is not always the safest way to travel from one place to another.

As you're exploring remote areas of the island, pay attention to the creation and expansion of the storm, and avoid getting caught within it. In this case, even though the soldier is located along the edge of the island, his location happens to be within the initial safe zone.

During this match, the soldier chose to land near map coordinates D9, but then had to quickly travel a far distance to get into the safe zone once the storm began to form.

Choosing to land along the outskirts of the island often requires you to travel far distances once the storm forms, in order to remain within the safe area. If you stay in the remote area for too long, make sure there's a vehicle (or another transportation method) you can use to quickly outrun the storm, since you likely will not be able to outrun the storm on foot.

Landing in a remote location gives you a lot of extra time to safely explore and build up your soldier's arsenal, while preparing for the End Game (the final few minutes of the match), without having to enter into combat early on. Avoiding combat will slow down your ability to boost your player Level within the game, but it'll help you stay alive longer during each match.

Building and Managing Your Arsenal

One of your most important responsibilities during every match is to help your soldier find, collect, and manage the most powerful arsenal possible. Based on the overall gaming strategy you adopt, where you are on the island, and what challenges your enemies confront you with, your arsenal needs will change throughout each match.

#13—Ways to Find and Grab Weapons

As you're exploring the island, there are several ways to find, grab, and collect weapons (along with ammo and loot items). In many places, both indoors and outdoors, you'll find weapons, ammo, and/or items lying on the ground, out in the open. As you can see here, this soldier is about to grab a Shadow Bomb and add it to his arsenal.

Each time an enemy is defeated, everything they were carrying in their own arsenal gets immediately dropped to the ground and available for others to grab. This is a great way to quickly improve your soldier's arsenal, especially toward the middle or end of a match, since the soldiers you'll be fighting would have had time to build up their own arsenal. It's always best to defeat an enemy after you know they've expanded their inventory, so you can benefit from whatever they've already collected.

Golden chests are scattered throughout the island. Some are in random locations, while others tend to be in the same place during every match. Chests contain a random selection of weapons, ammo, and loot items. They also give off a golden glow and make a unique sound, so they're easier to locate. Always approach chests with caution, in case an enemy soldier is hiding somewhere waiting to attack anyone who gets close.

Loot Llamas and Supply Drops appear randomly during matches. A Loot Llama looks like a colorful piñata and contains a collection of powerful weapons, ammo, and loot items. A Supply Drop, which also contains a random selection of goodies, looks like a wooden crate with a balloon attached to it. These fall from the sky.

Supply Drops can be seen from great distances as they drop to the island. As a result, it's common for multiple soldiers to approach them. When a battle ensues, only the surviving soldier will gain access to the loot inside the Supply Drop.

Chests, Loot Llamas, Supply Drops, Loot Crates (drones), and Vending Machines can only be opened or used once per match, so to acquire what they contain, you'll need to be the first soldier to approach it.

#14—Seek Out Chests

After opening this chest, this soldier was able to grab a Heavy Sniper Rifle, ammo, and a few other awesome goodies, and immediately add them to her arsenal.

Some chests are located out in the open and are easy to spot. Others are located inside structures or are hidden behind walls, for example. Within a house, a chest is often found within its attic or basement, but occasionally within a bedroom as well.

Remember, you can't always see chests. Sometimes, you'll need to listen carefully for the unique sound they generate as you get close to one. In this case, a wall needed to be smashed before the chest could be seen. The sound generated by the chest when the soldier was close tipped him off about its location.

Some chests reappear in the same location match after match. As a result, try to remember where you found chests during previous matches, so you can easily return to those locations and hopefully benefit by finding another chest. Since chests can only be opened once per match, you'll definitely want to be the first soldier to approach and open each of them.

During those few seconds when a soldier is opening a chest, they cannot use a weapon, explosive, or other items. As a result, they're momentarily vulnerable to attack. This is a good time to target an enemy and shoot them. The same is true when a soldier is opening a Loot Llama, Supply Drop, or using a Vending Machine.

#15—From a Distance, Attack Enemies Who Approach Vending Machines, Chests, Loot Llamas, and Supply Drops

It's a common strategy for a soldier (using a long-range weapon with a scope) to hide at a distance from one of these objects, target the object, and then wait for an enemy to approach. As soon as the enemy steps within the scope's sights, the trigger is pulled and that soldier gets eliminated from the match.

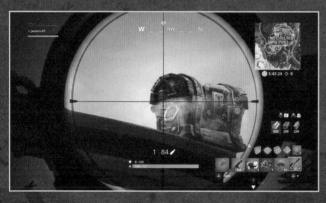

With a bit of planning and by choosing a good place to hide (that offers a clear line of sight to the object), it's relatively easy to defeat enemies. Just be careful you're not controlling the soldier who winds up in the crosshairs and who gets shot by enemies stalking you.

#16—Improve Your Arsenal Using Vending Machines

Vending Machines are scattered randomly throughout the island. Upon approaching a Vending Machine, you'll see what weapons or items are available from it based on what's displayed. You can only select one weapon or item to acquire. Once a Vending Machine is used once, it self-destructs.

Vending Machines tend to offer powerful weapons or very useful loot items. Each offers a different selection, so if it's safe and you spot a Vending Machine during your island exploration, approach it and see what's being offered. When deciding what to redeem, choose wisely, since you can only select one item.

For added protection when approaching and opening a Vending Machine, Supply Drop, or Loot Llama consider building metal walls around it and your soldier. If you're concerned about attacks from above, also build a roof on the protective cube.

#17—Don't Forget to Collect Ammo

Collecting a well-rounded selection of guns and weapons is important for achieving success when playing *Fortnite: Battle Royale*. The weapons you include within your soldier's inventory need to be able to help you win battles, regardless of the combat situation.

Anytime your soldier is exploring indoors (within a structure or building, for example), and you encounter an enemy, close-range combat will be required. Having at least one close-range weapon (such as some type of Pistol or Shot Gun) on-hand will be useful. Whether your soldier is inside or outside, mid-range weapons tend to be the most versatile, and will likely be used the most frequently.

Most Pistols and SMGs use Light Bullets, while Shotguns use Shells (shown here).

When you're far away from your enemy, a long-range weapon with a scope will allow you to very accurately target your enemy, while a long-range explosive projectile weapon (such as a Rocket Launcher, Grenade Launcher, or Quad Launcher, for example) can be shot from a distance and be used to defeat enemies and destroy objects (such as buildings, vehicles, structures, or fortresses).

Sometimes, ammo can be found lying on the ground, out in the open, either alone or with a compatible weapon.

Each type of weapon utilizes either Light Bullets, Medium Bullets, Heavy Bullets, Shells, or Rockets. Without having an ample supply of ammunition on hand for the weapons in your soldier's arsenal, those weapons will be useless. Collect ammo whenever and wherever you can!

Chests, Loot Llamas, and Supply Drops are also sources of ammo. Plus, whenever you defeat an enemy soldier, you have the opportunity to grab some or all of the ammo that the defeated soldier leaves behind.

Scattered throughout the island are Ammo Boxes. These green boxes do not make a sound or have a glow (like chests), but they do contain a random assortment of ammo. You'll often find Rockets within Ammo Boxes. This type of ammo can be found elsewhere, but it tends to be scarce.

Look for Ammo Boxes on the ground and on shelves (within buildings). They're sometimes found on their own but can occasionally be found close to chests. If it's safe, always take the time to open and grab ammo from Ammo Boxes, as it's a quick and easy way to replenish your stash. Running out of bullets during a battle is one of the worst mistakes you can make when playing *Fortnite: Battle Royale*.

#18—Get to Know Your Ammo

Light Bullets *are typically used in smaller, handheld weapons, such as Pistols and some SMGs.*

Medium Bullets *cause more damage than Light Bullets. These are typically used within Assault Rifles and work particularly well when used at mid-range.*

Heavy Bullets *are used mainly in Sniper Rifles. This are the highest caliber ammo available on the island, and useful for reaching long-range targets. Weapons that use Heavy Bullets tend to have a low fire rate and long reload time but cause the most damage per shot when a direct hit is made.*

#19—Manage Your Soldier's Inventory

Rockets are a projectile and explosive type of ammo that get shot from a Rocket Launcher, Quad Launcher, Grenade Launcher, Boom Bow, or Guided Missile Launcher, for example. This type of ammo can be shot from a distance. It then explodes upon impact. Not only are Rockets useful for inflicting major damage on enemies, they can also be used to easily and quickly destroy structures or objects. Rockets are most commonly found within Ammo Boxes, as well as chests, Loot Llamas, and Supply Drops.

As you find and grab weapons and loot items, pick and choose what you want to carry and have available, and then from the Inventory screen (shown here), rearrange the order of the items as needed.

Shells are used in various types of Shotguns. These weapons work well against close- to mid-range targets for a few reasons. For example, when a Shell is shot from a Shotgun, the ammo splits apart into many tiny pieces. When those pieces hit one target, each piece of the shrapnel causes damage. If two targets are at close range, pieces from a single Shell can hit and injure (or even defeat) multiple targets at once.

The drawback to a Shotgun that shoots Shells is that if you're too far away from your target when shooting this weapon, the Shell fragments have time to spread out a lot. Less of the ammo will hit your intended target, which means each hit causes much less damage. Plus, the farther away you are from your target when using a Shotgun, the less accurate your aim will be.

Some gamers opt to place their favorite type of gun in the slot to the immediate right of the Harvesting Tool (the slot on the extreme left). They use the next one or two slots for their next most commonly used weapons, and then insert one or two loot items (such as a Health or Shield replenishment item) in the right-most Inventory Slots. (A slot for the Harvesting Tool is displayed on some gaming systems, but not others.)

From the Inventory screen, use the Move or Drop commands to rearrange what's in each Inventory Slot as needed.

During firefights, keep your eye on the amount of ammo within the gun you're using. Each weapon takes a different amount of time to reload, during which time, you cannot fire that weapon. Knowing that you'll need to reload your weapon, choose a place you can duck behind for protection, such as behind a barrier or wall. When a weapon runs out of ammo, the message, "Not Enough Ammo" appears near the center of the screen, plus your soldier will shake their head when you try to shoot.

#20—How to Rearrange What's in Inventory Slots

Whenever you pick up a new weapon or loot item, it automatically gets placed within an available Inventory Slot. Your soldier's Inventory Slots initially fill up from left to right.

During a match, it's a good strategy to rearrange the items in your inventory so your most powerful and frequently used weapons and items are placed in the left-most slots.

In most situations, it makes little or no sense to carry around two of the same weapon, since inventory space is limited, and you want to have a well-rounded selection of weapons available. However, one instance when you might want to carry duplicate weapons is if you have a favorite weapon that has a small Magazine Size and slow Reload Time.

By placing the two identical weapons in Inventory Slots directly next to each other, instead of waiting for one weapon to reload when it runs out of ammo, you can quickly switch to the other (identical weapon) and keep firing. You're often able to switch weapons faster than it takes to reload a weapon—especially if you're using a Sniper Rifle that only holds one round of ammo at a time, for example.

How to Improve Your Aim and Shooting Accuracy

There are several ways to utilize almost every type of gun available in *Fortnite: Battle Royale*. Plus, the more you understand about each weapon's strengths and weaknesses, the more of a tactical advantage you'll have during combat.

#21—Shoot from the Hip

When using almost any type of gun (such as the Suppressed Pistol shown here), if you simply point the gun in the direction of your enemy and pull the trigger to shoot, this is referred to as shooting from the hip. It takes less time to set up the shot, but your aim won't be too accurate unless you're at close range. In some cases, there won't be time to properly aim your gun and shoot, so you'll need to rely on shooting from the hip to get some shots off.

#22—Use the Aim Feature

Most guns offered on the island, including the Suppressed Pistol, have an Aim feature. When you press the Aim button before pulling the trigger, you're able to more accurately aim at your target. When shooting at soldiers, always go for a head shot to cause the most damage. When using a weapon's Aim feature, it takes a bit longer to set up shots, but you'll notice a dramatic improvement in the weapon's targeting accuracy.

Anytime you're using a weapon with a scope, when you press the Aim button, the Scope View will be displayed. This allows you to accurately target enemies from a great distance.

#23—Pay Attention to the Size of the Targeting Box

Whenever you point a gun at a target, you'll see aiming crosshairs (also known as a Targeting Box) appear over that target. The size of this box will vary, based on your soldier's movement while aiming the weapon. In general, when you shoot a weapon, the bullets will land somewhere within that hit box.

To ensure a direct hit that'll cause maximum damage, you want the targeting box to be as small as possible when aiming your weapon. This can be achieved by standing still, crouching down, and pressing the Aim button for the weapon before pulling the trigger.

#24—Not Moving Will Improve Your Aiming Accuracy

The shooting accuracy of virtually all guns available on the island improve dramatically when your soldier is standing still, as opposed to walking, running, jumping, or moving when aiming the weapon.

To achieve the best aiming accuracy when shooting almost any gun available on the island, have your soldier crouch down, stand still, and then use the gun's Aim button before pulling the trigger.

#25—Understand How Weapons Are Categorized and Rated

As you know, at any given time, there are more than 100 different types of weapons available in *Fortnite: Battle Royale*. Each time a game update (patch) is released, or at the start of a new season, new weapons are sometimes introduced, while some weapons get vaulted. Others have their capabilities tweaked.

A weapon that is vaulted gets removed either temporarily or permanently from the game's Solo, Duos, and Squads game play modes, but those weapons will likely still be available in other game play modes, such as Playground, Creative, or the temporary game play modes released by Epic Games.

When a weapon gets "nerfed," this means that its power or capabilities are decreased by the game's programmers. However, sometimes a weapon's capabilities get "tweaked," which could improve its capabilities when used during a match.

Weapons are ranked based on color. Legendary weapons (with a gold hue) are the most powerful.

Epic weapons have a purple hue.

Rare weapons have a blue hue.

Uncommon weapons have a green hue.

Common weapons have a grey hue. Common weapons are the least powerful.

All guns are also rated based on their DPS (Damage Per Second) rating, Damage Rate, Fire Rate, Magazine Size, and Reload Time, for example.

During a match, you may be able to grab what looks like two identical guns, but one is ranked as Legendary and one is ranked as Rare, for example. The Legendary version of the weapon will be more powerful. The Legendary weapon will typically have a better DPS rating, Damage Rating, faster Fire Rate, a larger Magazine Size, and/or a faster Reload Time.

#26—Always Try to Achieve a Height Advantage

It's always easier to accurately target enemies with a gun when your soldier has a height advantage. This might mean climbing to the roof of a building, building a ramp to get higher than your opponent, or having your soldier stand on an object.

As you're entering into the End Game portion of a match, for example, if there's a hill or mountain in the safe area, try to reach the top of it, and then build your fortress to gain even more height.

Also during the End Game, when the safe circle gets really small, you may find yourself directly above or below your enemy. The soldier who is higher up almost always has the tactical advantage, so plan your strategy accordingly.

The soldier at ground level has a disadvantage since he's lower. On the plus side, this soldier has a long-range weapon with a scope and is hiding behind a large tree which provides some shielding.

Not only does being higher up improve your chances of successfully shooting an enemy, it also gives you a broader view of the surrounding area, so you can see enemies approaching from all directions.

#27—Keep Your Shields Charged for Added Protection

In addition to using Health-related items to keep your soldier's Health meter at 100 percent, there are also Shield-related items used for activating and replenishing your soldier's Shield meter. At the start of a match, a soldier's Shield meter is at zero. Shields can be activated by consuming a Small Shield Potion, Shield Potion, Mushrooms, Slurp Juice, or Chug Jugs, for example.

The more your Fortnite: Battle Royale gaming strategy relies on participating in combat, the more essential Shields are, since they offer added protection against incoming attacks and will help your soldier stay alive longer. It's always a good idea to boost Shields to 100 percent before a battle, and to replenish your soldier's Shields immediately after a battle.

It takes a few seconds to use or consume most Shield-related items, during which time your soldier must stand still. They can't simultaneously use a weapon or build, so they're somewhat vulnerable to attack. As a result, it's best to consume or use a Shield-related item when you know your soldier is safe from enemy attacks.

Fortnite: Battle Royale's Shield-Related Items

SHIELD ITEM	HOW LONG IT TAKES TO USE OR CONSUME	POWERUP BENEFIT	STORAGE LOCATION	MAXIMUM NUMBER YOU CAN CARRY
Chug Jug	15 seconds	Replenishes your soldier's Health *and* Shield meters to 100.	Requires one backpack Inventory Slot.	1
Chug Splash	Instant	Boosts your soldier's Health by 20. If their Health meter is full, their Shield meter gets a 20 point boost.	Requires one backpack Inventory Slot.	6
Coconuts	Almost instantly	Increases your soldier's Health meter by 5 points per Coconut that's consumed. However, if your soldier's Health meter is at 100, their Shield meter will receive some replenishment.	Coconuts must be consumed when and where they're found. They cannot be carried and used later.	None
Mushrooms	Almost instantly	Increases your soldier's Shield meter by 5 points (up to 100).	Mushrooms must be consumed when and where they're found. They cannot be carried and used later.	None
Shield Potion	5 seconds	Replenishes your soldier's Shield meter by 50 points (up to 100 maximum).	Requires one backpack Inventory Slot.	2
Slurp Juice	Approximately 2 seconds to consume and 37.5 seconds to achieve its full benefit.	For 37.5 seconds, a soldier's Health *and* Shield meters increase by one point (up to 75 points) every half-second after drink is being consumed.	Requires one backpack Inventory Slot.	1
Small Shield Potion	2 seconds	Replenishes your soldier's Shield meter by 25 points.	Requires one backpack Inventory Slot.	10

#28—Use Your Surroundings for Cover

The island where matches take place features many different types of terrain. Within each area, you'll discover buildings, structures, and natural surroundings (such as trees, vehicles, and rock formations) that your soldier can hide behind and use as shielding from incoming attacks, especially when they need to take a few seconds to use Health-related items, Shield-related items, or reload a weapon.

Crouching down and hiding behind a large rock formation will provide some protection against incoming attacks, because you'll be a smaller target that's harder for enemies to see and aim at.

While it's possible to hide within a large bush or behind a haystack and stay out of sight when enemies are in close proximity, bushes and haystacks offer no shielding protection whatsoever. Incoming bullets will easily penetrate bushes and destroy haystacks. As a result, if you know an enemy is nearby, especially during an End Game, but you can't locate them, try shooting or tossing explosives into nearby bushes.

Anytime your soldier is exploring inside of a house, building, or structure, the furniture or machinery inside can be used for protection, simply by crouching down behind it.

A broken down vehicle can also be used for protection, but not from all sides. Thus, it's important to keep tabs on where your enemies are, so you can anticipate from which direction(s) attacks might come.

#29—Quickly Build Structures for Shielding When Necessary

Learning to quickly build during a match is a separate skillset you'll want to master. While in Building mode, your soldier can use different-shaped building tiles to construct structures and fortresses. To be able to build, your soldier must first collect and harvest resources, including wood, stone, and metal.

There are four different building tile shapes you can work with, including: horizontal floor/ceiling tiles, vertical wall tiles, ramp/stair-shaped tiles, and pyramid-shaped tiles. Each tile type can be constructed using wood, stone, or metal. Mix and match the building tiles to create custom-designed structures and fortresses. Shown here are floor/ceiling tiles made from wood, stone, and metal.

Wood is the fastest material to build with but is the weakest in terms of offering any type of protection against attacks. Stone is stronger than wood but takes more time to build with. The strongest building material at your disposal is metal. It takes the longest to build with.

The following chart shows the maximum HP for each type of building tile you can work with. Keep in mind, Epic Games has tweaked this information multiple times in the past, so when you play *Fortnite: Battle Royale*, the HP strength of each tile may vary.

Ramps and bridges should be constructed using wood, since they typically won't need to offer protection, and it's important to build this type of structure quickly, especially when you're engaged in combat and need to establish a height advantage over your enemy, or your soldier needs to travel to the top or bottom of a hill, mountain, or structure quickly.

TILE SHAPE	WOOD	STONE	METAL
Horizontal Floor/Ceiling Tile	140 HP	280 HP	460 HP
Vertical Wall Tile	150 HP	300 HP	500 HP
Ramp/Stairs Tile	140 HP	280 HP	460 HP
Pyramid-Shaped Tile	140 HP	280 HP	460 HP

Here, from left to right, the vertical wall tiles have been constructed from wood, stone, and metal, respectively.

When a ramp/stair-shaped building tile is selected, a ramp is automatically created when wood is used. Stairs are created when either stone or metal is used.

Pyramid-shaped tiles can be used as a roof of a building or structure or placed within a building or structure to provide a protective barrier or additional shielding from incoming attacks.

Each building tile has its own HP meter. When that tile's HP meter hits zero, as a result of being damaged from a Harvesting Tool, weapon, or explosive attack, that tile will be destroyed. A soldier has the ability to repair a damaged tile (which requires additional resources). As damage is inflicted on a building tile, it will become translucent and its HP meter will decrease. Several shots have been fired on this brick (stone) wall. Its HP meter is currently at 162 out of 300. When a tile is translucent (meaning it's been damaged), you can see through it; however, your enemies can see through it as well.

Using the Editing tools available while in Building mode, it's possible to build a window (shown) or door, for example, into a vertical or horizontal building tile. When you do this, the maximum HP for that tile will be reduced slightly.

If your soldier is being shot at and you need to build a quick structure for protection, first build a horizontal wall-shaped tile out of stone or metal. Immediately behind it, build a stair tile, also out of stone or metal. Your soldier can now crouch down behind the stairs. An incoming attack will first need to go through two building tiles before reaching your soldier.

#30—How to Build a 1x1 Fortress

There will be times when you need to build a quick and easy fortress for protection and/or to give your soldier a height advantage during a battle. To build a 1x1 fortress, start by placing one floor tile on the ground. It's best to build this type of structure out of stone or metal.

From inside the structure, build four vertical wall tiles around the floor tile to create the first level of the fortress.

Within the fortress, build one ramp/stair tile. As it's being built, jump onto the ramp/stairs.

Build four additional wall tiles to create the second level of your fortress.

Keep adding as many levels as you deem necessary. Then, along the top of your fortress, add at least four pyramid tiles around the outer edges, and place a horizontal ceiling tile in the center. Never forget to build a roof

on your fortresses and structures to prevent an enemy from achieving a height advantage over your structure and then being able to drop explosives down into it from above or being able to shoot at you from above while you're hiding within the structure.

Once the shell of the 1x1 fortress is completed, use the Editing functions offered while in Building mode to add doors and/or windows to the structure as needed.

On the top of the structure, over the flat ceiling tile, you can place a Launch Pad to help your soldier make a quick escape, if needed, or place a Cozy Campfire item (used to replenish their Health meter). A 1x1 fortress can be built almost anywhere on the island, including on top of existing structures (such as a house or building) or on top of a hill or mountain.

#31—Use Ramps to Your Advantage

Using wood, building a ramp is a quick process that allows your soldier to travel upward. A wooden ramp was built here to help the soldier on ground level quickly travel upward so he could jump into the Slipstream.

Instead of building a ramp that faces a hill or mountain, consider building a ramp along the edge of that hill or mountain for added stability.

One drawback to building a tall ramp is that an enemy can shoot and destroy just one tile near the bottom of the ramp and the whole thing will come crashing down along with whoever is standing on the ramp. A fall from less than three levels won't cause too much damage, but a fall from higher up will often be fatal.

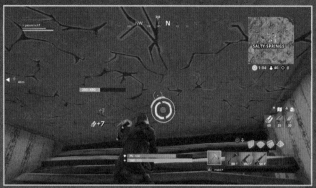

Ramps can be built inside existing structures. In this case, a ramp was built from the inside, so the soldier could reach the ceiling, smash through it using his Harvesting Tool, and then gain access to the house's attic.

#32—Build Over-Under Ramps for Added Protection

As you're building a ramp and traveling along it, if you need protection from a potential attack originating from above, consider building an over-under ramp. This allows you to simultaneously place a ramp-shaped building tile below your soldier's feet and over their head. This type of ramp requires twice the resources to build, but the added protection is often worth it. Point the building cursor directly forward (in front of the soldier) as opposed to toward their feet to build an over-under ramp.

#33—Construct Bridges to Maintain a Height Advantage

Be creative when building bridges between two or more structures. If necessary, build walls and a ceiling (shown here) to prevent attacks from the sides or above while crossing the bridge.

Using horizontal floor/ceiling tiles made from wood, stone, or metal, bridges can be constructed to make it faster and easier to cross over bodies of water, or to travel from one building or structure's rooftop to another while staying high above the ground. Building bridges made from wood typically makes the most sense.

Whether on foot or driving certain vehicles, traveling through lakes will often slow down your soldier. By building a bridge over the water, traveling across the body of water is faster and safer. If an enemy starts shooting, it's easy to build a protective barrier on a bridge. If you're traveling directly through a large body of water, your soldier will be out in the open, vulnerable to attack, and forced to travel at a slower pace. Building a bridge can eliminate these problems.

#34—You Can Shoot and Destroy Most Objects

Just about every object on the island, whether it's a tree, rock formation, vehicle, building, or structure, has its own HP (Hit Point) meter. Using the Harvesting Tool, an object made from wood, stone, or metal can be harvested to collect that resource.

Whenever an object's HP meter hits zero, it will be destroyed and disappear. You can see an object's HP meter by having your soldier face it. This soldier is using his Harvesting Tool to collect metal by smashing at a large truck. The truck's HP meter is reduced with each whack. As you can see, the HP meter is currently at 550 out of 600.

Damage to an object's HP meter can be caused by multiple swings from a Harvesting Tool, with bullet hits from a gun, or as a result of an explosion. Using explosives is typically the fastest and easiest way to blow up and destroy an object. Unless you use a Harvesting Tool to destroy something, you will not collect resources (wood, stone, or metal) from it.

Showcase Your Soldier's Explosive Personality Using Explosives

In addition to guns, at any given time, *Fortnite: Battle Royale* gives you access to a selection of throwable explosive weapons. These can be used to injure or defeat enemies, as well as to destroy almost any type of object (including buildings, fortresses, vehicles, and structures) in the game.

As you'll discover, each type of throwable explosive weapon has its own set of advantages and disadvantages. In general, throwable explosives, including Grenades and Dynamite, are mid-range weapons.

#35—Using Explosives to Destroy Buildings

Since most explosives, including Grenades (shown here), will bounce off of a solid object, such as a wall, it's best to throw or shoot an explosive weapon through a building, fortress, or structure's open door or window. Keep in mind, some explosives take a few seconds to detonate after they reach their target.

If your soldier is too close to the detonation of an explosion they themselves caused, they too will be injured.

#36—Destroy Buildings from a Distance Using an Explosive Projectile Weapon

Explosive projectile weapons, such as Rocket Launchers, Grenade Launchers (shown here), Boom Bows, and/or Quad Launchers, allow you to shoot explosive ammo from a distance and hit a target with extreme precision. Keep in mind, Rockets from a Rocket Launch can penetrate and destroy a solid wall, but Grenades from a Grenade Launcher will often bounce off a solid wall. When using a Grenade Launcher aim so you shoot through an open door or window, so the Grenade lands inside the structure and causes damage from within.

#37—Manage Explosives in Your Soldier's Inventory

Rockets are the ammo used by Rocket Launchers, Grenade Launchers, and Quad Launchers, for example. Each one of these weapons (when they're offered within *Fortnite: Battle Royale*) requires one Inventory Slot.

There are several types of throwable explosive weapons, each of which requires a separate Inventory Slot. Typically, when you find and grab a specific type of explosive weapon, such as Grenades or Dynamite, you'll receive a bundle of them at once. That entire bundle of the same weapon can be held in a single Inventory Slot. Once your inventory of that weapon is used up, the Inventory Slot will be empty and another weapon or item can be placed within that slot. This soldier is currently carrying four different types of throwable explosives.

By looking in the bottom-right corner of the screen at her inventory, you can see she's holding two sticks of Dynamite, three Impulse Grenades, six regular Grenades, and six Stink Bombs.

At any given time, a soldier can typically carry up to 10 of the same type of explosive weapon within one inventory slot. This, however, varies depending on the type of explosive weapon. From the Inventory Management screen, you can also see how many of each explosive item your soldier is carrying and move them around between Inventory Slots to make them easier to access when needed. It's also possible to Drop or Share throwable explosive weapons.

#38—Some Throwable Weapons Can Distract, But Do No Damage

Some throwable explosive weapons, like Grenades and Dynamite, cause an explosion which will inflict harm to an enemy caught in the explosion, and damage or destroy any objects within the blast zone of that weapon.

A growing number of throwable weapons don't cause an explosion. For example, a Stink Bomb creates a cloud of toxic yellow smoke. For every half-second a soldier gets caught in this toxic cloud, their Health meter gets reduced by 5 points. It's best to detonate this type of weapon within an enclosed space, so it takes longer for the enemy to exit the area, which results in more damage.

Other types of throwable weapons (like a Boogie Bomb) render an enemy soldier incapacitated for a few seconds, during which time you can launch other types of attacks to inflict damage, while some (like a Shadow Bomb) are used to make an undetected escape from an area or create a distraction. When detonated, an Impulse Grenade (shown here) will catapult an enemy away from the explosion and leave them disoriented for a short period.

A Shadow Bomb is not really a weapon at all. When used, it makes the soldier who detonated it almost invisible and able to run quickly for six seconds. This is useful when you want to rush an enemy and maintain an element of surprise, or when you need to make a quick retreat from an enemy and don't want to be easily followed.

Round Up of *Fortnite: Battle Royale*'s Throwable Weapons

During each gaming season, as new weapons and items are introduced into the game, others get vaulted. As a result, not all of these throwable weapons will be available at all times when playing a Solo, Duos, or Squads match.

THROWABLE WEAPON	DAMAGE	MAXIMUM NUMBER YOU CAN CARRY	STORAGE LOCATION
Boogie Bombs	Once detonated (by tossing it at an enemy), this bomb causes a soldier to dance uncontrollably for 5 seconds. During this time he or she is defenseless against other weapon or explosive attacks.	10	Requires one backpack Inventory Slot.

(Continued on next page)

THROWABLE WEAPON	DAMAGE	MAXIMUM NUMBER YOU CAN CARRY	STORAGE LOCATION
Bottle Rockets	This is a throwable fireworks weapon that works at mid-range. Once detonated, 45 rockets explode over a 9-second period. How much damage is caused depends on how close an enemy is to the explosion and how many rockets he or she is hit by. This weapon can also damage a structure that it's detonated in.	Pick up two Bottle Rockets at a time and store up to six within your soldier's inventory. Toss multiple Bottle Rockets at the same target to increase the destructive power. This item makes a lot of noise when detonated, so it attracts attention.	Requires one backpack Inventory Slot.
Clingers	Up to 100 HP damage can be caused if a soldier or object is caught in the explosion. Use this to defeat enemies or blow up objects or structures.	10	Requires one backpack Inventory Slot.
Dynamite	A throwable weapon that detonates 5 seconds *after* hitting its target. An explosion can cause at least 70 HP damage to a soldier and up to 800 HP damage to a structure.	10	Requires one backpack Inventory Slot.
Grenades	Up to 105 HP damage can be caused if a soldier or object is caught in the explosion. Use this to defeat enemies or blow up objects or structures. Unlike Dynamite, for example, Grenades detonate immediately upon impact.	10	Requires one backpack Inventory Slot.
Impulse Grenades	When thrown at enemies, this special Grenade will catapult an enemy soldier away from the explosion's point of impact. This item does not damage structures or objects.	10	Requires one backpack Inventory Slot.

THROWABLE WEAPON	DAMAGE	MAXIMUM NUMBER YOU CAN CARRY	STORAGE LOCATION
Remote Explosives	Damage to enemy soldiers varies, based on how close a target is to the explosion. If placed on a structure or object, it will blow it up. Use multiple Remote Explosives together to create a bigger bang.	10	Requires one backpack Inventory Slot.
Shadow Bomb	Allows the soldier who detonates this item to become invisible for six seconds. It's a great item to use if your soldier needs to make a quick retreat during a battle. It's also great for rushing (approaching) an opponent and being undetected until the last second.	6	Requires one backpack Inventory Slot.
Shockwave Grenades	When tossed, this type of Grenade will send whoever is in its path flying backward. This is more powerful than an Impulse Grenade but causes no actual damage when a soldier lands from their fall.	6	Requires one backpack Inventory Slot.
Stink Bombs	Once tossed, a Stink Bomb generates a toxic cloud of yellow smoke that lasts for 9 seconds. For every half-second an enemy is caught in the smoke, they receive 5 HP damage. This weapon works best when deployed in a confined area.	4	Requires one backpack Inventory Slot.

#39—Certain Explosives Take a Few Seconds to Detonate

Some types of explosives detonate the second they hit a target. Others, like Dynamite, take several seconds to detonate. This delayed explosion could give your enemies a few seconds to retreat if they see the explosive item being tossed or shot in their direction. It's important to learn how each type of explosive or throwable weapon works and understand how quickly they'll detonate. This soldier is about to toss two sticks of Dynamite through the partly open garage door, so the Dynamite explodes within the house.

Five seconds after the Dynamite landed at its target, it exploded and destroyed almost the entire first floor of this house. Remember, Grenades explode immediately upon impact. Dynamite takes a few seconds after it's been tossed to explode, so choose which one to use based on the situation at hand.

#40—For Distant Targets Use a Projectile Explosive Weapon Instead

Just like a gun that's equipped with a scope can be used to accurately target an enemy from a great distance, a projectile explosive weapon can be shot (with extreme accuracy) from far away, yet still cause a lot of damage and destruction if the weapon is used correctly. Remember, a Rocket Launcher can blast through and destroy solid objects, while Grenades shot from a Grenade Launcher, for example, will bounce off of walls and objects. It's best to shoot these through an open door or window when aiming at a building, structure, or fortress.

Launching Successful Ambushes & Surprise Attacks

Learning to use all the weapons at your disposal will help you defeat more enemies during each match, and potentially stay alive longer. Instead of constantly engaging in close-range combat, take advantage of your long-range weapons so you can have your soldier hide and then launch accurately aimed, perfectly timed attacks from a distance.

#41—Be Unpredictable!

Anytime your soldier is traveling out in the open, instead of walking or running in a straight line, follow an unpredictable zig-zag pattern and keep randomly jumping to make your soldier a moving target that's more difficult to hit.

Traveling in an unpredictable pattern also applies when using any type of vehicle, such as a Hoverboard. Keep making random turns and use the vehicle's Boost feature (when applicable) to alter your traveling speed.

Acting in an unpredictable manner is also essential when engaged in battles. Don't keep using the same weapon or the same attack methods over and over. Your adversaries will quickly learn your patterns and be able to easily predict and defend against what you'll do next. The more unpredictable your actions are, the harder it will be for enemies to defend against your attacks.

#42—Use a Weapon with a Scope to Launch Surprise Attacks

When you spot a chest, Supply Drop, or Loot Llama off in the distance, this is a great time to pull out your soldier's long-range weapon with a scope. While staying a good distance from your target, find a place to hide that offers a clear line of sight to your target, and then aim your weapon at the chest, Supply Drop, or Loot Llama. Wait for your enemy to approach the item and appear within your sights, and then start shooting.

#43—Look for Creative Places to Hide Before Attacking

Choosing to rush an opponent takes guts. When you do this, you're giving up the potential safety of your current location that's a safe distance from your enemy and choosing to quickly approach them in order to launch an attack. This strategy works best if you catch the enemy by surprise and can approach their location undetected until your bullets start flying. Prior to rushing an enemy, find a safe place to hide and replenish your soldier's Health and Shield meters. Then choose the perfect time to leave your safe haven and launch your attack.

#44—Shoot Enemies as They Exit Buildings

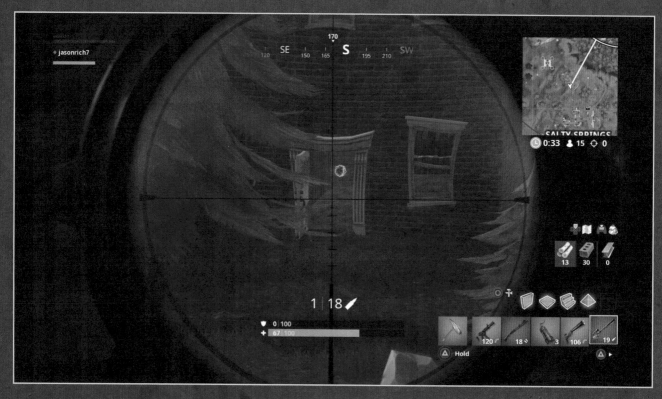

From a sniper's perch located a distance from a building where enemy soldiers are looting, for example, you're often able to shoot enemies who are inside a building by aiming through a window. Another option is to use a weapon's scope to target the door of a building or structure and wait for the enemy to leave. By waiting for the enemy's exit, you give them time to first collect whatever weapons, ammo, and loot items are within that building. Then, when you defeat that enemy, everything they were carrying drops to the ground and is now yours to collect.

While outside of any building or structure, listen carefully for the sounds of enemies inside. You might hear footsteps, doors opening or closing, the noises generated by an enemy's Harvesting Tool as they're gathering resources, or the sound of building.

If you approach an open door, don't go directly inside (like you see on the left). Someone could be waiting inside to shoot you. Instead, sneak up on the open door, approach from the side (shown on the right), and peek in to see if the coast is clear before entering.

#45—Target Enemies in Neighboring Buildings or Structures

Especially when inside of a building that's close to other structures or buildings, it's possible to shoot at enemies within those neighboring buildings using a long-range weapon and aiming it through a window. If you're on the second or third level of a building, aiming at an enemy on the second or third level of a nearby building, it's often possible to establish a clear line of sight and eliminate enemies with relative ease.

#46—Target Moving Vehicles, Not the Drivers or Passengers

Some vehicles, like Hoverboards, allow soldiers to transport themselves quickly around the island, but offer little or no protection/ shielding from incoming attacks. Other vehicles, like Quadcrashers and Ballers, for example, do offer some protection for the soldier(s) inside those vehicles.

When shooting at enemies that are traveling in vehicles, it's often easier to shoot at and attempt to disable or destroy the vehicle, as opposed to accurately target the soldier(s) within the vehicle. Consider using a projectile explosive weapon (such as a Rocket Launcher) to blast a moving vehicle or use a long-range weapon to shoot at it.

#47—Hide Inside Buildings and Wait for an Enemy to Approach

While inside of a building or structure, if you determine enemies are also inside that same structure and you'll need to engage in close-range combat, consider hiding behind objects within the building and positioning your soldier to launch a surprise attack.

Crouching behind furniture or objects offers protective shielding, however, positioning your soldier at the top of a staircase or around a sharp bend in a hallway, for example, provides an ideal location to attack from. Just make sure your soldier has an appropriate close- or mid-range weapon (with plenty of ammo) on hand and ready to fire.

#48—Set Traps Where They Can't Easily Be Spotted

Every gaming season, Epic Games makes a nice selection of Traps available. Some Traps can be placed on any flat surface (such as a wall, ceiling, or floor). If an enemy steps on or activates the Trap, they'll instantly be injured or defeated. Other Traps are designed simply to slow down an enemy or provide a way for any soldier to quickly travel away from a specific area.

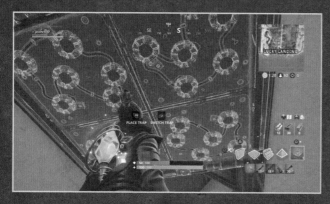

When placing a Trap that's designed to harm or defeat an enemy, choose a location that won't easily be spotted, such as on a ceiling near the entranceway to a building or structure. If an enemy spots a Trap that's been set, they can either avoid it, or shoot at it multiple times to destroy it before it can detonate. The trick to using Traps successfully is for them to achieve the element of surprise.

Unlike other types of weapons, Traps do not require one of your soldier's Inventory Slots. They are still collected and stored within your soldier's inventory, but to access and use them, it's necessary to switch to Building mode, and then select the Trap.

Once a Trap is selected, choose where you want to place it. If the outline of the Trap is displayed in red, this means you've selected a location that won't support the Trap. Choose an alternate flat surface or consider building a floor/ceiling tile or wall tile to place

the Trap on. Anytime you've gathered more than one type of Trap, after entering into Building mode, you'll be able to scroll through the different Trap types and choose which one to place, before choosing a location for it.

#49—Shoot from Above, Not Below

Regardless of whether you're fighting inside or outside, or what type of terrain your soldier is in, always try to establish a height advantage when you're about to engage in a mid-range or long-range firefight. In *Fortnite: Battle Royale*, it's easier to target enemies (and your accuracy will be better) when you're higher than them.

In this case, the soldier is standing on a crate found within an outpost. Anyone who enters the building or comes through the doorway won't see her hiding. Notice the soldier holding the weapon is pre-aiming her weapon (from above) near the center of the doorway. As soon as an enemy enters, she'll be in the perfect position to fire a few shots and take out the enemy before they can fire back or retreat.

#50—Attack Structures Without a Roof from Above

Anytime you need to attack enemies who are hiding within a fortress or structure they've built, always determine if there's a roof on that structure. Many gamers forget to add a roof when building a structure or fortress. This creates a major vulnerability. Instead of rushing the structure from ground level, build a ramp or figure out a way to get up higher than the enemy's structure, and then shoot downward into that structure. You can also toss explosives into the structure from the top of it (if there's no roof) or shoot an explosive projectile weapon from above.

Another attack strategy when approaching a structure that has no roof is to drop a few Stink Bombs into the structure from above. It'll likely take the enemies inside that structure a few seconds to exit, during which time you can launch additional attacks. You can also target the enemies as they're frantically leaving the structure to avoid exposure to the poisonous gas.

Especially during the End Game, when soldiers are building fortresses for protection, always look for weaknesses in the structure (such as the lack of a roof) and exploit it. Another vulnerability is when the enemy builds a tall ramp, and you can simply shoot at one of the bottom tiles of the ramp to destroy the entire ramp (with the enemy soldier still on it).

During those few seconds a weapon is reloading (assuming your soldier is carrying enough compatible ammunition to reload that weapon), your soldier will be vulnerable. It's best to crouch down (to make your soldier a smaller target) and then hide behind a solid object during the reload process.

#51—Keep Moving to Avoid Retaliation

Anytime you're able to catch an enemy by surprise, launch a few direct hits with your weapon, but not cause enough damage to defeat that enemy, after shooting the first few bullets (or while waiting for your weapon to reload), quickly take cover behind a solid object or move quickly to another location to avoid retaliation. It will likely take an enemy a few seconds to figure out where an incoming mid-to-long range attack originated from, so during those few seconds, quickly change your position.

Depending on the weapon, instead of waiting for a weapon to reload, it's sometimes faster to switch to a different fully loaded weapon that's already in your soldier's arsenal. Get to know the reload time for the various weapons you'll be using, so during an intense combat situation, you can quickly determine whether it's safer and more efficient to reload the weapon your soldier is using or switch to a different weapon.

#52—Get Comfortable with Your Weapon's Reload Time

Every type of gun in *Fortnite: Battle Royale* has a specific Magazine Size, which determines how many bullets it can hold at once. Each gun also has a pre-determined number of shots it can fire per second, whether you quickly press and release the trigger or hold down the trigger.

Once you've used up all of the ammo within the gun's magazine, it's necessary to reload the weapon. How long this reload process takes varies greatly, depending on the weapon.

If you've become highly proficient using a specific type of weapon that you know has a long reload time, consider collecting two identical weapons and storing them side-by-side within your soldier's inventory. This way, instead of waiting for the one weapon to reload, you can quickly switch to the other. Notice that the two Inventory Slots on the left both contain a Combat Shotgun. The Epic (purple) and Rare (blue) versions of this weapon both have a Magazine Size of 10, but the Epic version has a higher Damage rating (77 versus 73).

#53—Don't Run Out of Ammo

Of course, you always want to ensure that you enter into a firefight with plenty of compatible ammo for the weapons you plan to use. Running out of ammo during a combat situation is one of the worst mistakes you can make and will often result in your soldier getting defeated.

Ammo can and should be collected whenever possible during a match. There are multiple ways to find and gather ammo. Opening Ammo Boxes (like this one found in the attic of a house), chests, Loot Llamas, and Supply Drops often contain multiple large bundles of different ammo types.

Navigating Around the Island without Getting Lost

Depending on the gaming season, which *Fortnite: Battle Royale* game play mode you're experiencing, and where on the island your soldier happens to be exploring, your options for getting around the island will vary.

Of course, your soldier can always, walk, run, jump, or tiptoe around the island to get from location to location and avoid the storm, but this is not the fastest or most efficient way to travel—especially when you have to cover a lot of distance quickly.

Regardless of how you're getting around the island, there are specific strategies for giving your soldier an edge when it comes to winning firefights and staying alive as you're traveling on foot, versus riding in a vehicle, soaring through the air, riding Ziplines, or traveling within Slipstreams, for example.

#54—Practice Using the Newest Transportation Options

At the start of Season 9, for example, many parts of the island were equipped with a network of Slipstreams. Allowing your soldier to enter into the air flow within these Slipstreams offers a quick way to travel around parts of the island. These tubes are in addition to the network of Ziplines that were added to parts of the island in a previous gaming season. Each time a new method of transportation or a new vehicle type is added to the island, practice using it! Discover its strengths and weaknesses, so when confronted with specific situations or terrain types on the island, you'll have no trouble getting around quickly and safely.

In some cases, you'll need to build a ramp to get high enough to jump into a Slipstream.

As you explore the island, you will find these Slipstream stations where you can leap into a Slipstream directly from the platform. Once within the Slipstream, you can float within it as long as you'd like to travel from one location to another. When you're ready, use the Jump button or left/right directional controls on your controller or keyboard/mouse to exit from the Slipstream.

While in the Slipstream, use your directional controls to change the direction your soldier is traveling in. Keep in mind, if an enemy spots you whizzing by within a Slipstream, they can shoot at you. An opponent who's good at accurately shooting moving targets could take you out. It's not possible to use a weapon while traveling within a Slipstream.

#55—The Pros and Cons of Driving a Quadcrasher

Out of all the vehicles offered on the island, a Quadcrasher is probably the most durable, maneuverable, and versatile. It can travel across any type of terrain—including through water. Its HP meter maxes out at 500 HP, so it can take a lot of damage before it's destroyed. Unlike an All-Terrain Kart (ATK), it's very difficult to damage a Quadcrasher while driving it. Crashing into objects may slow it down, but it'll cause no damage to the vehicle. As long as your soldier remains within the vehicle, he too will receive no fall damage, unless hit by a bullet or explosion.

The Quadcrasher has a built-in Boost feature that takes a few seconds to recharge in between uses. With each boost, the rocket in the back of the vehicle ignites, and the Quadcrasher shoots forward at an ultra-fast speed. Use this to smash through larger objects, drive up a particularly steep hill, or to travel faster along flat terrain.

A Quadcrasher can also drive up a ramp and use it as a jump to go airborne for a few seconds. The landing will always be safe. Of course, it can also climb some steep hills and rock formations. While it's difficult to destroy (or even damage) a Quadcrasher while driving it, these vehicles can be damaged or destroyed by incoming gunfire or explosive weapon attacks. They also make a lot of noise, so they can be heard approaching from a distance.

After going airborne in a Quadcrasher, the landing might be a bit rough. Your soldier won't be harmed, but you could flip the vehicle.

As its name suggests, while driving a Quadcrasher, which holds a driver, plus passengers (when playing a Duos or Squads match, for example), the vehicle can crash through objects. The faster it's going, the larger the object it can smash through. Use the directional controls on the keyboard/mouse or controller to go in virtually any direction, including up, down, left, right, or directly over cliffs or ramps (in order to go airborne).

Before exiting a Quadcrasher (or any vehicle for that matter) first come to a complete stop. Otherwise, your soldier will jump off the vehicle, but the vehicle will keep moving forward for a few seconds.

A Quadcrasher is the perfect vehicle for quickly outrunning the storm (or escaping from the storm), because it moves really fast and can go virtually anywhere. If you happen to flip over a Quadcrasher or ATK, you'll need to exit out of the vehicle, face it, and then press the Flip button on your keyboard/controller in order to reposition the vehicle upright. You can then hop back in and start driving. A vehicle typically flips over as a result of a weird landing.

If you try driving up a steep slope (such as a rock mountain) and the Quadcrasher loses traction and starts slipping downward, hit the Boost button. A Quadcrasher can also travel through water, but if it's deep, your travel speed will be slowed down, and you could wind up being an easy target for nearby enemies—especially if they're armed with a Sniper Rifle (or weapon with a scope) or a projectile explosive weapon, such as a Rocket Launcher, Grenade Launcher, Quad Launcher, or Boom Bow.

#56—Get Things Rolling When Riding a Baller

While you're driving a Baller, it can crash into or smash through almost anything, such as a rock formation, mountain, building, or structure, and receive zero damage. Likewise, your soldier will receive zero fall damage if you drive off a cliff, for example. What can damage a Baller, however, are direct hits from an enemy's weapons. But, this vehicle can withstand a lot of damage before it gets destroyed.

As a Baller's HP starts to dwindle, you'll start seeing cracks in the ball. These can't be repaired. Try to find a safe location where your soldier can exit the vehicle and then defend himself using the weapons in his arsenal. You don't want the Baller to be destroyed while you're out in the open and vulnerable to attack, with no place to take cover.

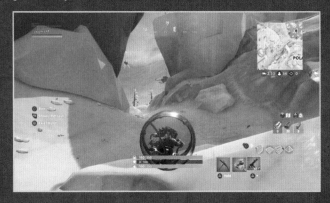

Unfortunately, while driving a Baller, your soldier cannot use a weapon and shoot at enemies. You can potentially crash directly into an enemy while traveling at a high speed or use the vehicle's grappling hook on them. Ballers are great for evading enemies and quickly travelling from one location to another, regardless of the terrain. On the plus side, a Baller is much quieter than an ATK or Quadcrasher, for example, so you can be stealthy when traveling around.

A Baller is particularly useful for outrunning the storm or escaping from it if you get caught within the storm. Keep using the Boost feature to speed up the vehicle and help you leave the storm faster so your soldier's HP suffers less damage.

A Baller's Grappling Hook can be shot from the vehicle, latched onto another object, and then used to quickly draw the Baller toward that object. The more creative you are when using this tool, the more maneuverable the vehicle will be, especially if you need to reach high-up locations where the vehicle can't simply roll. With practice and perfect timing, use the Baller's Grappling Hook to swing from tree to tree in a forest area, or use it to launch onto something overhead and pull the vehicle upward.

#57—Go Up, Up, and Away Using Balloons without Crashing Back to Land

At the start of Season 9, Balloons were vaulted from Solo, Duos, and Squads matches, but could make a return at any time. They continue to be available in some other game play modes, including Creative and Playground.

Balloons are a loot item. They can be found within chests, lying on the ground (out in the open), within Loot Llamas, in Supply Drops, and are sometimes offered by Vending Machines. Each time you pick up a Balloons item, it contains 10 Balloons that your soldier can carry and then use as needed. Once the stash of Balloons has been used up, this item disappears from your soldier's inventory and frees up a slot.

Once you add Balloons to your soldier's inventory (they take up one Inventory Slot), at any time you can activate one, two, or three balloons at the same time. One Balloon is shown here. When a Balloon is strapped onto your soldier's back, any time they jump, they'll go higher and travel farther, but slowly.

Activate two Balloons at once, and your soldier will be able to jump extra high. This is useful if you need to go from ground level to the top of a tall building or mountain, for example. While airborne, use the directional controls to move your soldier around and cover more distance (in addition to going up and down).

Anytime you activate three Balloons at the same time, your soldier automatically floats upward . . . and keeps going up . . . until you pop one or more of the Balloons or your soldier reaches a maximum possible elevation. At the same time, use the directional controls to move around. Using multiple Balloons allows you to reach high-up locations, or travel great distances while airborne, but the travel time is slow (compared to other transportation options). On the plus side, using Balloons generates no noise.

With three Balloons on your soldier's back, you'll fly very high up. Once you reach a certain altitude, however, one Balloon will automatically pop, so your soldier will level off. Use the directional controls to proceed to your desired destination. While up very high, you should be out of range from most (but not all) enemy weapons. An enemy with good aim and a Sniper Rifle will still be able to pick you off, even if you're up very high.

One drawback to Balloons is that they're brightly colored and can be seen by enemies from a distance. They don't make any noise, however. While airborne, it's possible to use any of your soldier's weapons, so you can shoot in a downward direction at your enemies, but they can shoot back.

If an enemy pops all of your soldier's Balloons while high up in the air, your soldier will come crashing down to the ground and perish. So, if you have good aim and are comfortable using the weapon(s) in your soldier's arsenal, using Balloons while enemies are nearby is fine. However, if you're a newb, save this item for when enemies are not nearby and there's little risk of your soldier getting shot down.

While airborne, to travel back down toward land, pop one Balloon at a time. If you're using three Balloons to float high up in the air but pop all three at once while still high up, you'll freefall back to land and perish. When using three Balloons, pop one, drift down a bit, and then pop the second. Wait to pop the third until you're very close to land or have safely landed. When using one or two Balloons at once, the downward directional control can be used to help your soldier land, but it'll be a slow descent.

It's possible to travel around the island—on the ground—and always wear one Balloon. This, of course, it literally putting a bright-colored target on your back, but it allows your soldier to leap higher and farther anytime when using the Jump command.

When your soldier wears Balloons and uses a Hoverboard, for example, he can float through the air or glide along the ground's surface. Talk about having options!

#58—Hoverboards Offer a Great Transportation Option for One Soldier

This is typically the fastest moving and most maneuverable type of vehicle available on the island. It works on any terrain and allows your soldier to float just above the ground. While riding a Hoverboard (also called a Drift Board), your soldier can use whatever weapon they're carrying, so you can shoot and move at the same time. Aiming and hitting targets while traveling at a high speed is relatively difficult, however.

The most awesome thing about a Hoverboard is that it's indestructible. While an enemy can shoot at your soldier and injure or defeat them, the vehicle itself will often remain undamaged. This is a one-person vehicle. However, in some locations, if you're playing a Duo or Squads match, for example, you'll discover multiple Hoverboards in one location, so your partner or each squad member can grab one and you can all travel together.

A Hoverboard can be used to outrun the storm or quickly escape from it. These vehicles can also travel almost anywhere, including up or down mountains, and directly over cliffs (so they go airborne). This is one of the few vehicles that you can use in conjunction with other items, such as Balloons, or a Health/Shield replenishment item. For example, when you're driving a Hoverboard and inflate two or three balloons, you can go airborne and take to the skies as you travel. You're still an open target that enemies can shoot at, and the Hoverboard will be a bit less maneuverable, but this is always an option.

Gliding over water, snow, or ice, for example, is all quick and easy. Very little can slow down a Hoverboard. When going at medium or high speed, be gentle with the directional controls to maximize your maneuverability and control.

Like most vehicles on the island, anytime you come across a Hoverboard, you can hop on it and start driving. When you stop the Hoverboard and hop off of it, your soldier cannot pick it up, add it to their inventory, and take it with them. It'll stay where it is until you return to that location or another soldier commandeers it.

Thanks to its speed and maneuverability, a Hoverboard can go virtually anywhere on the island, including up or down ramps, with ease. This is also a very quiet vehicle. Unlike other vehicles, you do not need to hop off of a Hoverboard in order to open chests and collect what's inside them. You can also interact with other items, weapons, and tools you encounter.

#59—Go Airborne Using a Glider Item

Unlike vehicles that you'll find parked at various locations around the island, a Glider is actually a loot item that your soldier can find, pick up, add to their inventory, and then activate when it's needed. Glider items can be found lying on the ground, out in the open. They're also sometimes found within chests (shown here), Loot Llamas, and/or Supply Drops, for example, or you can pick one off of an enemy soldier whom you've defeated. You might also discover a Glider item being offered from a Vending Machine.

Glider items are a bit tricky in that they can only be used in certain circumstances. First select the item from its Inventory Slot. You then need to have your soldier leap off of a high location, such as a mountaintop, cliff, or building's roof. At the exact right moment, activate the Glider. Your soldier can then glide through the air, travel horizontally across a great distance (depending on the height), and then land safely. However, if your timing isn't perfect, the Glider won't open in time, and your soldier will land with a splat.

While airborne, your soldier cannot use a weapon. Use the directional controls to navigate and choose a landing location, but keep in mind, your soldier can be shot at while airborne or while landing, so you may need to take some evasive maneuvers to avoid an attack.

Like a Bouncer Pad or Launch Pad, a Glider is an ideal tool if you need to escape (or relocate) from the top of a building or fortress quickly, such as during the End Game portion of a match. If you need to get to a high-up location quickly in order to deploy a Glider, build a tall ramp and then leap off it.

When Glider items are available during matches, they tend to be pretty common. They do, however, take some practice to use effectively and safely. Once you collect a Glider item, it can only be deployed 10 times before it disappears from your soldier's inventory.

Once a Glider is deployed successfully, control it in the same ways as you'd control your soldier's Glider during freefall after leaving the Battle Bus at the start of a match. Whichever Glider design you've selected for your soldier before a match will be the one that's used during the match in conjunction with the Glider item. All Glider designs function exactly the same way. The differences in appearance are cosmetic only.

#60—Take Advantage of a Vehicle's Boost Feature

To quickly, but temporarily pick up speed, use a Quadcrasher, Hoverboard, or Baller's Boost feature. This allows the vehicle to burst forward with a temporary increase in speed and power. Using this feature allows you to avoid enemy attacks, reach places that are otherwise inaccessible, or to help you confuse an enemy by traveling in an unpredictable manner.

#61—How to Attack a Moving Vehicle

Always listen for the sound of an approaching vehicle. You'll often hear it coming closer before you can see it. Once you spot an enemy driving a vehicle, you have four options:

1. Use your gun and start shooting. You can either aim for the driver and try to defeat them directly or aim for the vehicle and inflict as much HP damage

as possible. From a distance, using a Sniper Rifle (or weapon with a scope) works nicely, but you need to take into account that the vehicle is in motion, and aim accordingly. In other words, depending on your distance from the vehicle, aim slightly in front of it.

2. Attack a vehicle using throwable explosives. A Clinger will work really well, because it'll stick onto the vehicle and then explode. A Grenade can also work, but you need to toss it into the vehicle. If the Grenade hits the outside of a vehicle, it'll often just bounce off. The same is true with other types of throwable explosives, like Dynamite.

3. Take advantage of a projectile exploding weapon, such as a Rocket Launcher, Guided Missile Launcher, or Quad Launcher. Target the vehicle and blast it with one or two direct hits. Not only will this likely destroy the vehicle, but it'll typically defeat (or at least injure) whoever is inside. A Boom Bow can also be used to shoot explosive arrows at a moving target, such as a soldier in a vehicle. (Since the target will be moving, aim slightly in front of the intended target to account for the time it takes for the arrow to travel to its destination.)

4. Avoid the vehicle altogether and allow it to pass without a confrontation.

#62—Use a Launch Pad Item to Go Airborne

A Launch Pad is a loot item that can be found, collected, stored in inventory, and then used when it's needed to quickly catapult your soldier into the air.

Shown here, a Launch Pad has been placed on a flat surface. It's now ready for use, simply by stepping on it. The drawback to using this item is its setup time. If you're in a massive hurry, it's not always practical. Plus, if an enemy is following you, they can use the same Launch Pad right after you.

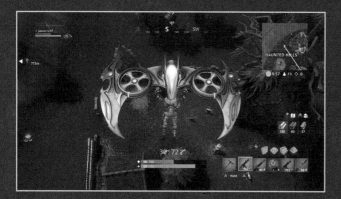

Once airborne, use the directional controls to navigate as your soldier falls back toward land. Their Glider will automatically deploy to ensure a safe landing. This is a useful tool for quickly reaching the top of a mountain, house, building, or structure.

A Launch Pad must be positioned on a flat surface. This often requires a solider to first build a floor tile (made of wood, stone, or metal) and then place the Launch Pad on top of it. Once it's been activated, it cannot be packed up and relocated. It can, however, be used an infinite number of times by any soldier, unless it's manually destroyed.

Unlike many loot items, a Launch Pad gets stored within your soldier's inventory with their resources (wood, stone, and metal) and ammo. Thus, it does not require an inventory slot. To select and activate a Launch Pad, your soldier must enter into Building mode, and then select the Launch Pad from the resources inventory. (The way you select, position, and activate it is identical to how Traps are used.)

#63—Whiz Through the Air on a Zipline

Depending on the gaming season, crisscrossing certain regions of the island you'll likely discover a network of Ziplines. To ride a Zipline, walk up to one end of it, look up, and press the Enter Zipline button on your keyboard or controller. Your soldier will quickly sail through the air to the opposite end of the Zipline.

While riding a Zipline, enemies can shoot at your soldier from the ground. However, they'll be able to shoot back while in motion. Anytime you're riding a Zipline, have a mid-range weapon in hand—preferably one with a large Magazine and quick Reload Time—and be ready to shoot.

Once your soldier latches onto a Zipline that goes up and down a hill or mountain, for example, they can travel in either direction, as often as they wish. As your soldier is riding a Zipline, use the directional controls to rotate around so your soldier can look or aim his weapon in different directions. It's also possible to slow down and stop the ride at any point, and even switch directions. (The direction your soldier is facing, related to the Zipline, is the direction he'll travel.) This can be useful if you're trying to shoot at an enemy below. It's always harder to accurately shoot at a moving target, so by stopping your soldier's travel along the Zipline, it may become easier to make a shot. However, as a non-moving target, this also makes it easier for your enemies to shoot at your soldier.

When a Zipline is not too far from the ground, if you want to exit the ride early, press the Jump button and your soldier will immediately fall to the ground. This can cause an injury (or be fatal) depending on the height, so be careful! At the end of a Zipline's route, your soldier will automatically jump off safely at the landing location.

#64—Avoid Crashes While Riding Ziplines

Keep in mind, if two soldiers are traveling on the same Zipline but in opposite directions, when they collide, both will fall to the ground. The red poles that hold up the Ziplines cannot be destroyed, so don't bother trying.

#65—Slipstreams Offer Another Way to Go Airborne

At the start of Season 9, Epic Games populated the island with a network of Slipstreams. These are like air tunnels that a soldier can travel within. By jumping into the fast moving air flow of a Slipstream, your soldier will be swept away and can glide through the air between locations.

While traveling within a Slipstream, use the directional controls to choose your travel direction. It's also possible to travel faster within the air flow, but doing this gives you less control, so you could wind up catapulting your soldier out of the air tunnel when trying to make a sharp turn.

Upon leaving a Slipstream, a soldier busts forward through the air. Their speed and travel direction depends on the angle they leave the air tunnel. A soldier can enter into a Slipstream on their own, or while riding in almost any type of vehicle.

#66—There Are Many Other Transportation Alternatives

In addition to many types of vehicles, and transportation structures that have been added to the island (like Ziplines and Slipstreams), there are natural phenomena on the island that allow soldiers to move around quickly, plus you'll have access to a selection of additional items that can be used for transportation.

In terms of natural phenomena, Rifts and Geysers (shown here) can often be found on the island. When your soldier steps into one of these, they'll go airborne and you can then navigate them to another location. (These natural phenomena come and go from the game, based on the gaming season.)

While they were not designed to be a vehicle, Loot Carrier drones can be stood on and used to transport your soldier around the island. You can't control their travel path, however. When you're done with the ride, destroy the drone to collect the weapon(s) and loot it's holding.

#67—No Matter How You Travel, Stay Out of Open Areas

Whether you're on foot or using another transportation method to get around the island, keep in mind your soldier can be attacked anytime they're out in the open. Pay attention to your soldier's surroundings at all times (including above and below, when applicable).

Items like a Grappler, Bounce Pad, or Rift-To-Go (shown here) can often be found, collected, stored within your soldier's inventory, and then used when needed to get around the island much faster than on foot. Regardless of which gaming season or game play mode you're experiencing, determine what transportation options are available, and then practice using them so you're able to get around the island, outrun the storm, avoid enemies, and explore quickly, safely, and efficiently.

Try to keep moving when out in the open and move in an unpredictable pattern. At the same time, if bullets start flying your way, be prepared to take cover behind an object. In some cases, the only protection available will be a simple structure you build yourself, so be ready to switch into building mode to, at the very least, build a wall or barrier out of stone or metal that your soldier can hide behind. Bridges can be challenging to cross if there's an enemy with a sniper weapon nearby because as your soldier crosses the bridge, there's often nothing to hide behind for shielding.

When traveling through open areas using a vehicle, take advantage of the vehicle's Boost mode to move faster. You're better off **not** following paved roads or clearly marked paths to get from one location on the island to another, since enemies will likely be watching these routes more closely.

Especially when out in the open, always be ready to contend with attacks from above or from the sides. An enemy could go airborne, be positioned on top of a building's roof, be waiting at the top of a mountain or hill, or quickly build a ramp to achieve a height advantage and then launch an attack. Shown here, the soldier is driving a Quadcrasher along a paved road through an open area. An enemy is shooting from the hillside above. Evasive maneuvers in conjunction with the vehicle's Boost mode should allow the soldier driving the vehicle to get through the area with only a few non-lethal hits.

#68—Use Firepits to Replenish Your Soldier's Health

In addition to Cozy Campfires, which are loot items that can be found, collected, stored within a soldier's inventory, and then used when needed, you'll discover Firepits scattered throughout

the island. These are often found at campsites. Have your soldier approach a Firepit, light the fire, and then stand near the flames in order to replenish some of their Health meter.

Like when using a Cozy Campfire, a soldier must stand still for up to 30 seconds to enjoy the full healing benefit of a Firepit, so make sure the area is enemy free, or be prepared for battle if an enemy approaches. Consider building metal walls around the Firepit and your soldier for added protection while the healing is taking place.

Avoid the Deadly Storm

Getting caught in the storm is detrimental to a soldier's health, depending on how long they stay engulfed within it.

#69—Some of the Best Gamers Are Storm Riders

A "storm rider" is a gamer who voluntarily enters into the storm-ravaged area of the island in order to execute a specific strategy. In some situations, it makes sense to voluntarily enter into the uninhabitable area of the island in order to reposition yourself to launch an attack against an enemy from behind, or to take a shortcut to a safer location. Using a transportation item to go airborne or traveling in some type of vehicle will reduce the amount of time you need to spend in the storm.

When a gamer positions their soldier near the edge of the storm (on the safe side of the blue wall), this often provides a better viewing perspective of the remaining battle area, especially during the End Game. Gamers that do this often focus their attention just on what's happening within the safe area and ignore the fact that an enemy could sneak up from behind and emerge from within the storm. Anytime you're near the storm's edge, be prepared to defend yourself from all directions.

Get to Know the Newest Terrain

Anytime new points of interest are added to the map, invest some time getting acquainted with that new area. There are several ways to do this. One of the most common ways is to participate in a Solo, Duos, or Squads match and choose to land in that new area at the start of a match and then do as much exploring as you can.

#70—Explore During Matches

Every gaming season, new points of interest are added to the map and some existing points of interest are overhauled. At the end of Season 8, for example, the infamous Tilted Towers location was destroyed and then as Season 9 kicked off, it was replaced by Neo Tilted, a futuristic-looking city. Shown here is what Tilted Towers looked like once it was destroyed, but before Neo Tilted took its place.

As you can see, Neo Tilted has taken on an all-new look and layout. Like any new major point of interest on the island, it'll take a typical gamer a bit of time to get to know the layout of the new area so they can use the terrain to their advantage, particularly during battles.

#71—Take Advantage of Playground Mode

Upon landing on the island when in Playground mode, you have just under four hours per session to explore. Use this time to get to know the terrain, experiment using different types of weapons, practice your building skills, and brush up on your driving skills when riding in different types of vehicles.

Instead of simultaneously having to explore new terrain and fight off enemies while avoiding the deadly storm, each time a new point of interest is added to the island, consider entering into Playground mode. Choose the new location as your landing spot once you're in Playground mode (either alone or with fellow gamers) and take the time to explore at your own pace.

To enter Playground mode from the Lobby, first access the Game Play Mode menu and choose the Playground option. If you want to visit this area alone, choose the Don't Fill option. Continue by selecting the Play option from the Lobby.

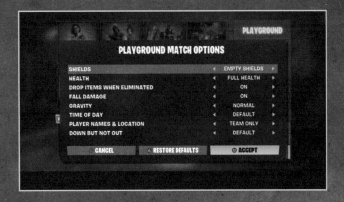

If you want customize your experience while in Playground mode, access the Playground Match Options menu after selecting Playground mode from the Game Play Mode menu. One at a time, select each menu option and choose the setting you desire. When you're done, return to the Lobby and select the Play option.

Choose one of the featured, gamer-created island maps and matches from the Hub, and then as your soldier freefalls toward the island, choose your landing location.

From the Playground Hub, turn 180 degrees to select a specific landing location on the island that offers default game settings. From here, you can freely explore any area of the island for up to four hours per session. This is the option to choose if you want to visit a new and unaltered point of interest on the map, explore at your own pace, and experiment with weapons and loot items without fear of encountering enemies or having to outrun the storm.

#72—Participate in a Temporary Game Play Mode to Learn New Terrain

On any given day, Epic Games offers several temporary game play modes. These limited-time modes change often and typically includes some type of 50v50 match. Instead of experiencing a situation where it's your soldier against 99 others, for example, when you play a 50v50 match it involves two teams consisting of 50 soldiers each.

A Team Rumble typically refers to a 50v50 match. A Team Rumble Squads match allows you to join a four-soldier squad, which becomes part of a 50-soldier team. This team competes against another 50-soldier team and must complete specific objectives during a match to achieve #1 Victory Royale.

In many cases, when the teams are given a specific goal, individual soldiers will automatically respawn in the match after being eliminated, or they can be respawned by other team members. Playing one of these matches gives a gamer extra time to explore new areas of the island, while their fellow team members can watch their back and help defeat enemies.

End Game Survival Tips: Those Last Few Minutes Really Count!

Preparation is the key when you enter into the End Game in hopes of winning a match. It's also important to stay calm, watch what your enemies are doing, and stay focused on your objectives.

#73—Choose the Best Location if You Decide to Build a Fortress

Based on the terrain where the final safe zone of the island is during the End Game, select the best location to build your fortress, from which you'll likely make your final stand in battle. If you're in a good position, you can be more aggressive with your attacks.

If you're in the dead-center of the final circle, your soldier will become the center of attention, which probably isn't good. Make sure your fortress is tall, well-fortified, and that it offers an excellent, 360-degree view of the surrounding area from the top level.

During this End Game, the soldier reached the top of a hill within the safe circle, and then built a small fortress on that hill to give herself an even bigger height advantage. Notice she's near the outer edge of the safe zone, so she can focus most of her attention toward the remaining safe area with her back to the storm's blue wall.

Should your fortress get destroyed or get engulfed by the storm, be prepared to move quickly, and have a backup strategy in place that will help to ensure your survival. Having the element of surprise for your attacks gives you a tactical advantage. Don't become an easy target to hit. Keep moving around your fort or while you're out in the open!

#74—During the End Game, Don't Engage Every Remaining Soldier

Sometimes it makes more sense to conserve your ammo and allow some of the remaining enemies to fight among themselves to reduce their numbers, plus reduce or even deplete their ammo and resources.

#75—Use a Sniper Rifle for Long-Range Shots

Only rely on a sniper rifle (or scoped rifle) to make long-range shots if you have really good aim and you're a distance from an enemy. Otherwise use explosive weapons (such as a Rocket Launcher) that'll cause damage over a wide area. There will be times during an End Game when you wind up very close to your remaining adversaries, so only close- or mid-range weapons will be useful. Even with some type of sniper rifle, aiming at a moving target can be tricky. Aim slightly ahead of your moving enemy to take into account the time it'll take for the bullet to travel from your soldier's gun to its target.

#76—Keep Tabs on the Location of Your Enemies

Don't allow enemies to sneak up behind you (or approach from above), for example, during an End Game. Even if your back is to the storm, an enemy could enter the storm temporarily, and then emerge behind you to launch a surprise attack if you lose track of their location.

#77—Only Build When Necessary

Don't invest a lot of resources into a massive and highly fortified fortress until you know you're in the final circle during a match. Refer to the map and the displayed timer. Otherwise, when the storm expands and moves, you could find it necessary to abandon your fort, and then need to build another one quickly, in a not-so-ideal location. Having to rebuild will use up your resources. Base pushers are enemies that aren't afraid to leave their fortress and attempt to attack yours during the final minutes of a match. Be prepared to deal with their close-range threat.

#78—Focus on One Enemy at a Time

If two or three enemies remain, focus on one at a time. Determine who appears to be the most imminent and largest threat. Be prepared to change priorities at a moment's notice, based on the actions of your enemies.

#79—Be Ready to Replenish Your Health and Shields

During the End Game, have a Chug Jug (or other Health- and Shield-related items) on hand to replenish your soldier's Health and Shield meters after they've been attacked. Find a safe place to hide before using an item that'll take seconds to consume or use, during which time your soldier will be vulnerable.

#80—Prepare for Close-Range Combat

In some End Game situations, the only recourse is to engage the final enemies in close-range combat. Sometimes, the remaining safe area is so tiny, your enemy will either be directly on top of or below you. Be prepared for this and use weapons that can defeat enemies and/or destroy the structure or object an enemy is standing on or crouching behind.

#81—Don't Fall without a Plan

Anytime you need to drop down from very high up, be sure to use a loot item, such as a Launch Pad, Bouncer Pad, Rift-to-Go, Glider item, or Grappler to ensure a safe landing. Going airborne while in a vehicle will also result in a safe landing. In some cases, as you're falling, you can quickly build floor tiles below your soldier to prevent a freefall to the ground. This, however, takes good timing and practice. Whatever you do, don't just jump from a height of more than three levels up, or your soldier will sustain damage or could be instantly killed. You can slide down a steep hill safely by pointing your soldier's feet toward the hill as they're sliding.

#82—Be Prepared to Make a Quick Retreat

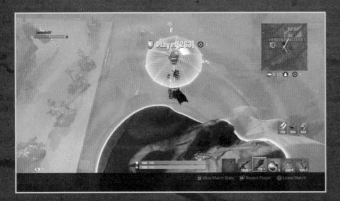

Using a Glider item, Launch Pad, Bounce Pad, Grappler, Rift-To-Go, or whatever transportation item is at your disposal, be prepared to make a quick retreat from your current location if you're confronted by an enemy whose arsenal is clearly more powerful than yours, or if your current position is not conducive to achieving a win. For example, if an enemy clearly has a height advantage, you don't have enough ammo on hand to defeat the enemy, or your soldier's Health meter is dangerously low already.

#83—Go into the End Game with Plenty of Resources

Not all gamers focus on building during the End Game, but if you do plan to do some building, it's a good idea to enter the End Game with at least 300 to 500 stone and metal, plus as much wood as you can collect (500 or more), since this is the material you'll mainly use for ramps, bridges, and other structures you need to build quickly. Once there are only a few soldiers remaining and the safe area of the island is very small, there will be very little time (or safe places) to harvest resources. You can, however, grab resources that eliminated enemies leave behind. It's possible for a soldier to carry up to 1,000 wood, 1,000 stone, and 1,000 metal at once.

#84—Shoot at Bushes to Lure Out Enemies Hiding within Them

Sometimes, an End Game will take place out in the open. There will be no place to hide and building a structure yourself will quickly reveal your location. In this case, consider hiding within (not behind) a large bush. You'll remain out of sight and can launch an attack if an enemy comes too close. However, savvy gamers know to shoot at bushes during the End Game when they can't locate their enemies. Bushes offer no protection against bullets or explosives whatsoever. They simply provide a place to hide.

#85—Practice the Art of Ultra-Fast Building

Some End Games require gamers to quickly build and repair fortresses or structures to gain a height advantage, to provide a place to hide, or for protection against incoming attacks. When your final adversaries are in very close proximity, the soldier who is able to build (and repair structures) the fastest, achieves a height advantage over their enemy, and then can switch to Combat mode to shoot the fastest will almost always win the match. Don't just practice basic building skills. Make sure you're able to build very quickly and are comfortable switching between Building and Combat mode at lightning-fast speed during a firefight.

#86—React Fast When You're Face-to-Face with an Enemy

When it comes down to just you and one or two other enemies during an End Game, the winner of the match will likely be determined based on who reacts the fastest when choosing an appropriate close-range weapon, and which gamer can target their moving enemy the most accurately. Of course, having a height advantage and making sure your soldier has ample Shields to withstand a few bullet hits will be beneficial. Despite all of the traveling around the safe zone, building, and relocating during the final moments of the match, the last two soldiers remaining wound up face-to-face—literally just a few feet apart—for their final duel.

#87—Sometimes It Makes Sense to Just Kick Back and Chill or Do Some Recon

During the End Game, if you find a safe place to hide, use it. Allow the other remaining soldiers fight each other and waste their ammo, while you take a few minutes to relax, replenish your soldier's Health and Shield meters, and think about your next attack strategy. Just make sure when you choose a hiding place that it's well within the safe zone. When the storm expands and moves again, and a few of the soldiers have eliminated each other, you can re-enter the match fully ready to face your next challenge.

Instead of just sitting still waiting for her enemies to find her, this soldier built a fortress, and then used a Launch Pad to periodically leap into the sky and do some reconnaissance in order to prepare for her final battles. This was useful to help her figure out the current location of the remaining four soldiers. The drawback was that she ran the risk of getting shot at while airborne. With full Health and Shield meters, this soldier could easily survive a few bullet hits.

Proven Duos and Squads Match Strategies

In addition to all of the responsibilities you have during a Solo match, when you participate in a Duos or Squads match, you'll also have additional tasks to juggle. For example, you'll need to communicate effectively with, and protect, your partner or squad mates.

#88—Choose a Landing Spot

While in the pre-deployment area or still aboard the Battle Bus, you and your partner should discuss where to land. If one or more players is not using a gaming headset and can't talk, everyone should place a Marker on the Island Map.

Some squads opt to land in different locations initially, and then meet up as the End Game draws closer. This strategy only works if all members of the squad are really good gamers and can hold their own against enemy squads that are traveling and working together. The benefit to separating is that each squad member can explore and loot a different area in order to build up their arsenal.

#89—Stick Together, But Not Too Close

Anytime you're traveling with your partner or squad mates, don't stay too close together. If you're too close and an enemy tosses or shoots an explosive weapon, you'll all wind up getting injured or worse if you're simultaneously caught in the blast radius. By spreading out a bit, it makes it much harder for an enemy to target you and your partner (or you and your squad mates) at the same time.

#90—Share a Vehicle

Some vehicles, like Quadcrashers, hold multiple soldiers at once. The benefit to riding together with a partner or squad mate(s) is that one person can drive, and the other passengers can shoot at enemies, use items, or build while the vehicle is in motion. In other situations, you may find one-passenger vehicles, like Hoverboards, clustered together, so multiple soldiers can then travel together.

Just like when traveling on foot, don't stay too close together. Leave space between the vehicles to help avoid incoming explosive attacks.

#91—Use Markers

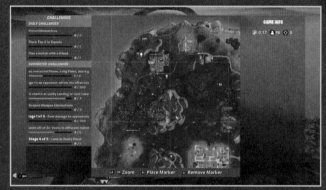

In addition to using a Marker to set and agree on a landing location, use Markers to set rendezvous points on the island if you and your partner, or you and your squad mates get separated. Markers can be seen by your allies from a great distance and appear as colored flares on the main game screen. Remember, your enemies cannot see Markers placed by you, your partner, or your squad mates.

#92—Take Advantage of the Compass

Displayed in the top-center of the screen is a compass. When telling a partner or squad mate the location of something, don't say things like, "ahead of me," "to my right," or "to my left." Unless the gamer you're speak-

direction as yours, these navigational directions will mean nothing and get confusing. Instead, use the compass to describe where things are or what direction to move in.

#93—Plan Coordinated Attacks

The biggest benefit of working with a partner or squad mates during a match is that you can pre-plan perfectly timed, well-coordinated attacks on your enemies. The more practice you have working together with other gamers, the easier it'll be to coordinate attacks quickly. When pre-planning an attack, be sure to discuss what each person's responsibilities are, where they should position themselves, and what their intended targets are. Be specific.

#94—Revive Your Partner or Squad Mates

Anytime your partner or one of your squad mates gets injured, but not defeated, try to safely approach and heal them during a match. Watch out for the enemy soldier that attacked them in the first place. They could still be lingering around.

However, when a partner or squad mates get eliminated, as long as it's safe to do so, grab their Reboot Card within 90 seconds and make a beeline for a Respawn Van. These vans are randomly located throughout the island. Once you have a Reboot Card in hand, bring it to a

Respawn Van to bring your fallen comrade back into the match.

#95—Beware of Attacks When Reviving Another Soldier

If your enemies determine your goal is to respawn a fallen soldier, they're more apt to closely guard the nearest Respawn Van, so approach it with caution and be prepared for an incoming attack.

#96—Share Weapons, Ammo, and Resources

Anytime you and a partner or squad mate are close together, if you want to share weapons, ammo, loot items, or resources, access your soldier's Inventory Management screen, select what you want to share, and then use the Drop command to drop the item(s) directly in front of the soldier you want to share with.

If you have multiples of the same type of ammo, loot item, or resources, for example, you can choose how much of that item in your possession you want to Drop and ultimately share.

#97—Watch Each Other's Backs

Anytime a soldier chooses to use a Health or Shield replenishment item, the process takes several seconds, during which time your soldier must stand still and cannot use a weapon or build. In addition to hiding in a safe place when using these items, when you're playing a Duos, Squads, or any type of team-oriented match, consider having another soldier guard your location with their weapon drawn to provide additional protection.

Likewise, if one squad mate is rushing an enemy or enemy fortress, it often makes sense for at least one or two allies to stay back and provide cover fire and a distraction using a long-range weapon or explosives. The more you can confuse an enemy about where attacks are coming from, the easier it'll be for the soldier who is rushing the enemy to get really close without being detected.

#98—Focus on Each Gamer's Strengths and Skills

If you're playing a Duos or Squads match with people you know, take the time to discover their strengths and weaknesses as a gamer. Determine what skills each squad mate has and which weapons they're most proficient using, so when assigning tasks, everyone is able to perform the tasks they're best at. This will give your squad a tactical advantage.

For example, when traveling with a squad, assign one soldier to gather resources and ammo, another to collect weapons, and have the remaining two stand guard and offer protection. When engaging in battle, define each squad mate's role. Assign one soldier to be a sniper (who is skilled at using a gun with a scope from a distance). Another soldier can handle explosives. A third soldier can provide cover fire or attack the enemy from the side, while the fourth soldier rushes the enemy head on.

Especially when playing a Squads match, well-coordinated attacks work best when fighting against four other soldiers. Of course, anything you can do to divide up and confuse an enemy squad will also work to your advantage.

#99—Have Your Soldiers Dress Alike to Intimidate Enemies

When participating in Squads matches with the same three squad mates over and over, consider dressing up your soldiers in identical outfits prior to a match. Anytime an enemy sees four soldiers dressed alike, this helps to intimidate them and gives the impression that the squad is highly skilled, experienced, and a true force to be reckoned with (or avoided).

Even when all four soldiers in a squad dress in the same outfit, each gamer can still choose a unique Harvesting Tool design or Back Bling design to differentiate themselves a bit, yet still look like you're part of a menacing squad.

#100—Learn by Teaming Up with Strangers

Instead of continuously playing with the same partner or squad mates, if you're looking to improve your gaming skills, consider playing with total strangers by selecting the Fill option after choosing the Duos or Squads game play mode. Especially if you and the strangers you're playing with all have gaming headsets, you can easily talk to each other during a match and learn from each other.

Anytime you're participating in a squad where the other gamers are clearly more skilled and experienced than you, follow them around and take their direction and advice as you proceed through the match.

Don't Get Ripped Off! Avoid *Fortnite: Battle Royale* Scams

Thanks to the worldwide popularity of *Fortnite: Battle Royale*, there are a growing number of online scams that are targeting gamers that you definitely want to watch out for.

#101—Only Purchase V-Bucks from the Store within the Game

As you know V-Bucks are the in-game currency used to acquire optional outfits, emotes, Battle Passes, and other items from the Item Shop. The only way to purchase V-Bucks (using real money) is directly from the game itself, by selecting the Store option. Never attempt to purchase V-Bucks from unofficial websites offering them for a discount.

If an online friend or stranger offers to give you *Fortnite: Battle Royale* outfits or trade outfits, do not ever agree to give someone your Epic Games account username or password (or the username and password used to access the online gaming service associated with your console-based gaming system).

There have been a growing number of incidents where a gamer gives someone else their username and password thinking that free outfits or other items will be transferred to their account, when in reality, the person offering the free gifts then takes over the account (by changing your password) and will often steal the credit card information linked with the account.

While exploring the Internet in search of *Fortnite: Battle Royale* information, beware of online-based "V-Bucks Generators." These fake websites will ask for your Epic Games account username and password, and potentially for your name, address, phone number, and credit card information, but will give you absolutely nothing in return. You're likely sharing your information with online criminals looking to perpetuate online fraud or identity theft. There is no such thing as a "V-Bucks Generator."

If you're a Fortnite: Battle Royale newb and still need to download and install the game onto your PC, Mac, PS4, Xbox One, Nintendo Switch, iPhone, iPad, or Android-based mobile device, be sure to use the download link provided by the official Epic Games website (www.epicgames.com/fortnite). Do not attempt to download the game from another site, unless it's the official online store associated with your gaming system.

SECTION 4

FORTNITE: BATTLE ROYALE RESOURCES

On YouTube (www.youtube.com), Twitch.TV (www.twitch.tv/directory/game/Fortnite), or Facebook Watch (www.facebook.com/watch), in the Search field, enter the search phrase "*Fortnite: Battle Royale*" to discover many game-related channels, live streams, and prerecorded videos that'll help you become a better player.

Also, be sure to check out the following online resources related to *Fortnite: Battle Royale*:

WEBSITE OR YOUTUBE CHANNEL NAME	DESCRIPTION	URL
Best *Fortnite* Settings	Discover the custom game settings used by some of the world's top-rated *Fortnite: Battle Royale* players.	www.bestfortnitesettings.com
Corsair	Consider upgrading your keyboard and mouse to one that's designed specifically for gaming. Corsair is one of several companies that manufacturers keyboards, mice, and headsets specifically for gamers.	www.corsair.com
Epic Game's Official Social Media Accounts for *Fortnite: Battle Royale*	Visit the official Facebook, Twitter, and Instagram Accounts for *Fortnite: Battle Royale*.	Facebook: www.facebook.com /FortniteGame Twitter: https://twitter.com /fortnitegame Instagram: www.instagram.com /fortnite
Fandom's *Fortnite* Wiki	Discover the latest news and strategies related to *Fortnite: Battle Royale*.	http://fortnite.wikia.com/wiki /Fortnite_Wiki
FantasticalGamer	A popular YouTuber who publishes *Fortnite* tutorial videos.	www.youtube.com/user /FantasticalGamer
FBR Insider	The *Fortnite: Battle Royale Insider* website offers game-related news, tips, and strategy videos.	www.fortniteinsider.com
Fortnite Config	An independent website that lists the custom game settings for dozens of top-rated *Fortnite: Battle Royale* players.	https://fortniteconfig.com

WEBSITE OR YOUTUBE CHANNEL NAME	DESCRIPTION	URL
Fortnite Gamepedia Wiki	Read up-to-date descriptions of every weapon, loot item, and ammo type available within *Fortnite: Battle Royale*. This Wiki also maintains a comprehensive database of soldier outfits and related items released by Epic Games.	https://fortnite.gamepedia.com /Fortnite_Wiki
Fortnite Intel	An independent source of news related to *Fortnite: Battle Royale*.	www.fortniteintel.com
Fortnite Scout	Check your personal player stats, and analyze your performance using a bunch of colorful graphs and charts. Also check out the stats of other *Fortnite: Battle Royale* players.	www.fortnitescout.com
Fortnite Skins	This independent website maintains a detailed database of all *Fortnite: Battle Royale* outfits and accessory items released by Epic Games.	https://fortniteskins.net
Fortnite Stats & Leaderboard	This is an independent website that allows you to view your own *Fortnite*-related stats or discover the stats from the best players in the world.	https://fortnitestats.com
Fortnite: Battle Royale for Android Mobile Devices	Download *Fortnite: Battle Royale* for your compatible Android-based mobile device.	www.epicgames.com/fortnite/en-US /mobile/android/get-started
Fortnite: Battle Royale Mobile (iOS App Store)	Download *Fortnite: Battle Royale* for your Apple iPhone or iPad	https://itunes.apple.com/us/app /fortnite/id1261357853
Game Informer Magazine's *Fortnite* Coverage	Discover articles, reviews, and news about *Fortnite: Battle Royale* published by *Game Informer* magazine.	www.gameinformer.com/fortnite
GameSkinny Online Guides	A collection of topic-specific strategy guides related to *Fortnite*.	www.gameskinny.com/tag /fortnite-guides

WEBSITE OR YOUTUBE CHANNEL NAME	DESCRIPTION	URL
GameSpot's *Fortnite* Coverage	Check out the news, reviews, and game coverage related to *Fortnite: Battle Royale* that's been published by GameSpot.	www.gamespot.com/fortnite
HyperX Gaming	Manufactures a selection of high-quality gaming keyboards, mice, headsets, and other accessories used by amateur and pro gamers alike. These work on PCs, Macs, and most console-based gaming systems.	www.hyperxgaming.com
IGN Entertainment's *Fortnite* Coverage	Check out all IGN's past and current coverage of *Fortnite*.	www.ign.com/wikis/fortnite
Jason R. Rich's Websites and Social Media	Learn about additional, unofficial game strategy guides by Jason R. Rich that cover *Fortnite: Battle Royale*, *PUBG*, *Brawl Stars,* and *Apex Legends* (each sold separately).	www.JasonRich.com www.GameTipBooks.com Twitter: @JasonRich7 Instagram: @JasonRich7
LazarBeam's YouTube Channel	With more than 11 million subscribers, LazarBeam offers *Fortnite: Battle Royale* tutorials that are not only informative, but very funny and extremely entertaining.	YouTube Channel: http://goo.gl /HXwElg Twitter: https://twitter.com /LazarBeamYT Instagram: www.instagram.com /lazarbeamyt
Microsoft's Xbox One *Fortnite* Website	Learn about and acquire *Fortnite: Battle Royale* if you're an Xbox One gamer.	www.microsoft.com/en-US /store/p/Fortnite-Battle-Royalee /BT5P2X999VH2
MonsterDface YouTube and Twitch. tv Channels	Watch video tutorials and live game streams from an expert *Fortnite* player.	www.youtube.com/user /MonsterdfaceLive www.Twitch.tv/MonsterDface
Ninja	On YouTube, check out recorded game streams from Ninja, one of the most highly skilled *Fortnite: Battle Royale* players in the world. His YouTube channel has more than 22 million subscribers.	YouTube: www.youtube.com/user /NinjasHyper Ninja recently left Twitch.tv and now streams live on the new Microsoft Mixer service (https://mixer.com/Ninja).

WEBSITE OR YOUTUBE CHANNEL NAME	DESCRIPTION	URL
Official Epic Games YouTube Channel for *Fortnite: Battle Royale*	The official *Fortnite: Battle Royale* YouTube channel.	www.youtube.com/user/epicfortnite
Pro Game Guides	This independent website maintains a detailed database of all *Fortnite: Battle Royale* outfits and accessory items released by Epic Games.	https://progameguides.com/fortnite /fortnite-features/fortnite-battle -royale-outfits-skins-cosmetics-list
ProSettings.com	An independent website that lists the custom game settings for top-ranked *Fortnite: Battle Royale* players. This website also recommends optional gaming accessories, such as keyboards, mice, graphics cards, controllers, gaming headsets, and monitors.	www.prosettings.com/game/fortnite www.prosettings.com/ best-fortnite-settings
SCUF Gaming	This company makes high-end, extremely precise, customizable wireless controllers for the console-based gaming systems, including the SCUF Impact controller for the PS4. If you're looking to enhance your reaction times when playing *Fortnite: Battle Royale*, consider upgrading your wireless controller.	www.scufgaming.com
Turtle Beach Corp.	This is one of many companies that make great quality, wired or wireless (Bluetooth) gaming headsets that work with all gaming platforms.	www.turtlebeach.com

Your *Fortnite: Battle Royale* Adventure Continues . . .

No matter how much of a pro you become playing *Fortnite: Battle Royale*, thanks to the weekly updates made to the game, and the dramatic changes you can expect at the start of each new gaming season, there's always something new to experience and new challenges to face. Plus, even if you become highly skilled playing Solo matches, for example, there are always other game play modes to try out, each of which offers a different twist to the ultra-intense battle royale combat experience.

Once you've mastered the strategies offered throughout this guide, which is going to take practice, plan on investing extra time exploring the island and getting to know the terrain, while at the same time, becoming proficient using the many different types of weapons, transportation options, and loot items available.

Especially if you're a newb, don't expect to start playing *Fortnite: Battle Royale* and achieve #1 Victory Royale right away, unless you happen to be a great gamer and get very lucky. Instead, focus on continuously increasing how long you can survive during each match, while also working to improve your success rate when shooting at enemies using different types of weapons.

There are two additional strategies that'll help you quickly improve your gaming skills when playing *Fortnite: Battle Royale*. First, learn to anticipate how your enemies (who are being controlled in real time by other gamers) will react in various situations. Study your adversaries during each match. Look for patterns in their actions and try to determine each player's weaknesses so you can exploit them.

Second, memorize the gaming controls you're using when playing *Fortnite: Battle Royale*, and develop your muscle memory for the game (and the controls your using) as quickly as possible. Doing this will improve your reaction time and allow you to focus more on the tasks at hand, instead of which button or key to press to accomplish a specific task.

Nothing replaces the need to practice! Aside from that, try to stay calm, even during the most intense combat situations, and don't forget to have fun!